The Power *of* Everyday Networking

Building Authentic Connections
throughout Your Career and Life

Patti Hunt Dirlam

with Perry McIntosh

CareerBridge Press

To my network

Visit www.huntdirlam.com to purchase copies of this book or to contact Patti Hunt Dirlam for speaking or workshop engagements.

Cover design: Rachael Tracy
Interior design: Anne L. Rolland

Printed in the United States of America
First printing: December 2011

ISBN: 978-0-692-01284-0

8 7 6 5 4 3 2 1

DEAR NETWORK,

A BOOK ON NETWORKING can only be written if you are fortunate enough to have and be part of a diverse, talented, generous, genuine and caring network, and I am. The journey of this book was long (ten years, in fact), but never lonely. Every step along the way, someone in my network was there to help me make this book possible. From the time I first thought, "Here is a simple, straightforward networking approach," to the final proofreading of *The Power of Everyday Networking*, so many friends and associates offered advice, feedback and guidance. They opened doors, provided research and shared stories. They listened to my dream, quieted my *can't do* fears and offered an encouraging smile when I would say, for the one hundredth time, "Well, I'm still working on it, but it's almost done." I thank each of you for your support and faith in me.

Every network has its core members, treasured over a lifetime and special in ways that words cannot explain. For me, this group includes Susan Kavanaugh, Mary Donnelly, MaryLou Northgraves, Cynthia Sullivan, Phyllis Meyer and Rosemary Waterman. My core group also includes my family and the friends who have made me and my husband, John, part of their families. Life has been rich and rewarding because of all of you.

There are a few other people I would like to mention as they represent the power of everyday networking and its impact on helping me write this book. First is Susan Chiumiento, whom I was fortunate to get to know and become friends with when I was working in Boston. Susan used her extraordinary administrative skills to transcribe my impossible-to-read handwritten notes. Another is Beth Berg, to whom I was referred by a former colleague when I was lamenting that I could not find anyone to transcribe some tapes. Beth magically turned dozens of tapes into hundreds of readable pages.

The book's cover was created by Rachael Tracy, a Boston-based graphic designer and the sister of a friend of my nephew Matthew. Matthew met Alex in college (1995); over the years, he and his family became part of my family's core network. We are eternally grateful for Alex's thoughtfulness and kindness.

What's written between the front and back covers is in large part due to Perry McIntosh. We first met in 2004 while Perry was a client after working twenty years in publishing. In 2010, when I decided to finally write the book that I had carried in my head and my heart for so many years, I asked around my network to see who could help me find a writer to put my voice to paper. Several people suggested I speak with Perry, so I called her to learn more about the publishing process. When I asked if she knew any good ghost writers, she replied, "Well, how about me?" Since that phone call in early 2010, Perry has gone from ghost writer to co-writer, project manager and networker extraordinaire. She introduced me to Katie Bull, who graciously offered expert advice and help on another part of writing a book: getting it professionally self-published, stored, sold, and shipped!

A book needs readers, and five members of my professional network volunteered to take time from their business lives to review the final draft. Their diverse backgrounds, experience and expertise provided me with ideas and feedback that strengthened the book in many ways. So, my thanks to: Jeff Brown, an architect, former client, and good friend who asked at our twice-a-year breakfasts, "When will I be reading your book?" Letty Garcia and Madelyn Sierra, fellow leadership coaches at Harvard Business School's Executive Education Program; Sarah Malinowski, a communication and media relations professional at Saint Peter's College in New Jersey, the niece of Mary Donnelly and someone I got to know while sitting on the beach in Kennebunkport, Maine; Cindy Connelly, a marketing professional and neighbor whom I know through the Boston Club. We share an occasional early morning coffee and when I mentioned looking for readers she immediately volunteered. Nancy Monson is a professional writer and editor in Connecticut, referred to me by Gail McMeekin, a nationally recognized career coach, author and thirty-plus-years' friend. Gail was the first to tell me "I had a book," and over the last ten years would check in "just to see how it was going" and to ask how could she help.

A special thank you to my husband, John. He is the one who has been there during the many ups and downs of my book-writing journey. He's been there through "I'm going to write this; I'm not going to write this." He has been there for the "Would you read this; would you proofread this;" and he has been there when he couldn't find a clean place to sit down for a meal because my piles of paper spilled from my desk onto the dining room table, kitchen table and every other space I could find. Most importantly, though, John has "been there" for me every day for the last thirty years, including the twenty-five years of our marriage.

CONTENTS

PREVIEW

LET ME TELL YOU about a recent week in my life. I flew to Washington, D.C., for a professional conference and some sightseeing with my husband. Before the conference kickoff, I enjoyed breakfast with a group of participants I had gotten to know at previous meetings. Like most people, I was tempted to hang around with my friends and catch up on their news during the conference. But I had made an investment in time and money to attend this event. So, knowing I would be more likely to meet new people if I wasn't busy chatting with old friends, I suggested to the group that we finish our breakfast and hit the sessions alone.

At the conclusion of one panel discussion, a woman at my table shared her unanswered questions with me. I encouraged her to approach the dais with her queries and, as I always do, I introduced myself and asked her name. I recognized it immediately; she was the coauthor of a highly influential book, one that had changed the lives of many people, including many attendees of that session! I asked what had brought her to the conference and, as we waited for the crowd at the head table to thin, we spoke about her career and her current professional focus. Before moving on to the next session, I introduced her to an acquaintance—an expert in the field she was currently pursuing. I was sure they would quickly discover many common professional and personal interests. Later, I shared a cab back to the hotel with a woman who, when I introduced myself, said, *What can I learn from this person?* "Oh, you're Patti Dirlam! Someone was just telling me that I should contact you for help with my job search." Small world, indeed! We made arrangements to talk later, and she (a Washington native) shared some must-see destinations in the city.

After sightseeing the next day, I approached the hotel concierge about a cab to the airport later that evening. "Why not hire a car?" he asked. "It will cost the same, and you can schedule it so you won't have to wait for a cab." I took his advice. On the ride to the airport that evening, I took the driver's business card to give to my neighbors, who planned to be in Washington the following weekend for a college graduation. They were grateful to have it and scheduled their pick-up with the same driver, avoiding long cab lines on the busy commencement weekend.

The flight home was full, and my husband and I shared our row with a well-dressed frequent flyer I'll call "George." After the usual small talk about weather-related travel woes, our conversation drifted to more personal interests. George was thinking about the next phase of his life and looking forward to it with a mixture of anticipation and dread. Having some knowledge of this topic after more than two decades in human resources and executive coaching, I shared some resources that I thought he might find useful. As the plane landed, George told me that he was a member of a large organization of highly placed executives, many of whom were facing the same issue. He gave me his card and urged me to call him and talk more about helping the members of his group.

That week was not unusual. Almost every week of my life has involved similar stories of brief and beneficial connections. It would be easy to dismiss these as pure accident or luck—after all, what are the odds that a well-connected executive would sit next to me and, even more amazing, that he would be seeking advice in my specialty? How likely is it that I would be able to introduce an author I have always admired to a person who could help her in her newest career venture? Or share a cab with a person who had heard good things about me from a friend of a friend and was planning to call me later? And what's the big deal about taking five minutes to help out a neighbor with a car at the airport?

Perhaps you're thinking that as a networking "guru," I simply know how to work a room. You may be thinking that I'm such an outgoing person that I naturally engage every stranger and that, just as all roads lead to Rome, all my conversations lead inevitably to my own professional needs or services. Or you may be thinking, "She's pushy, forcing her card into every hand she shakes and meddling in the lives of everyone she knows."

You'd be wrong on all counts. What makes these stories part of my normal day is what I call *authentic* and *everyday networking*. For some networkers—

I call them *transactional networkers*—the aim is to develop a list of contacts. This mechanical, transactional networking has developed a negative reputation. Transactional networkers think of their contacts when they need help or want to sell something. Authentic networkers don't wait until they need a network to start building one; their everyday actions create a network that is ready at all times.

To build this kind of network, we need to look at networking itself in a new way. We need to *redefine* networking. Let's drop those old "tell and sell" practices and develop a habit of authentic networking. Let's create strong relationships and turn contacts into connections, whether they are brief or long-term. Let's build the networks we deserve, learning the skills we need to support, maintain, and tap them as needed. And a robust and supportive network is only one of the many benefits of rethinking our approach to networking. Other outcomes include firsthand, new, and interesting knowledge on a variety of topics; access to the best professional services in your area; and everyday pleasant encounters that may or may not develop into acquaintances, friendships, or business opportunities.

What makes everyday networking special is the attitude and intention that its practitioners bring to every connection. None of the encounters in my week started with "Let's see how I can turn this conversation toward me and what I want." When I spoke to George on the airplane, my first intention was to cordially negotiate seat selection so that my husband and I could sit together. When I meet someone, my attitude is "What can I learn from this person?" So, I let George manage the level and topic of our conversation. Each of us had "plane work" available for a retreat if we chose, but our conversation developed naturally into a substantive one that just happened to touch on my professional life. Even if we had not found a topic of mutual professional interest, neither George nor I would have felt *stuck* in that airplane seat—we would both have been pleased with our good *luck* to be seated in the same row. The difference between *stuck* and *luck* is just one thing that makes authentic networkers special.

Authentic networking isn't a new idea, but its principles can be elusive in the rush of trying to "get somewhere" in the world. Redefining networking means embracing an apparent paradox: The more you give the more you receive. This timeless idea is set forth in literature from the Bible to *Grimms'*

Fairy Tales. But authentic networking is no fairy tale. Authentic networking is the way I have learned to make each encounter a pleasant experience and to learn from everyone I meet. Some people approach networking with a single-minded determination to collect names, numbers, and links. They believe it isn't worth the time spent getting to know anyone who can't help their current career or business goals. This book is not for them. This book is for people who want to extend their networks far beyond simple contact lists to genuine connections with helpful people who care about them. By opening themselves to serendipity and learning, everyday networkers reap a harvest of professional and personal rewards. They reach their goals, succeed at their quests, and enjoy the journey, every day. This book will show how you can do the same.

? This book is designed to help you develop a new way of networking by re-thinking your attitudes, approaches, and activities. To that end, it includes many opportunities for reflection. In each lesson, you'll see several mini exercises, each highlighted by a large question mark. You'll find more thought-provoking questions embedded in every chapter. Finally, each lesson ends with a set of "Questions for Reflection."

You may want to use a notebook to record your answers along with other thoughts as you examine yourself and your networking activities. I encourage you to return to these questions more than once—your answers may change over time as you bring authenticity to your networking. Reviewing your responses will be useful as you think about how to network more authentically every day.

WHAT IS EVERYDAY
NETWORKING?

TWENTY YEARS AGO, I was asked to speak on the subject of networking at a company's career development breakfast. As I waited to be introduced, I looked at the hundred or so attendees and thought about the many professional and personal connections they shared. Everyone in the room worked for the same organization and belonged to the association sponsoring the breakfast. Many knew each other from working together on projects or committees. All had interesting backgrounds and life experiences. So, I couldn't help wondering: "Why are so many of these people standing alone, reluctant to reach out and introduce themselves to those nearby?"

Moments before the networking workshop was scheduled to begin, more participants rushed in. Each scanned the room as if looking for an open seat, but passed several half-empty tables to sit beside a person who held up both arms in a big wave and pointed to an adjacent seat, as if to say, "I've saved this just for you!" I realized then and there that, although the mechanics of networking can be taught, networking as a way of life doesn't come naturally.

Most of us would agree on the importance of networking in job searches and career transitions. And most of us have experienced several career transitions. Research indicates that over the course of our five-decade career journey, most people change jobs rather frequently—with the average job lasting fewer than four years—and have numerous (from three to eleven!) major career transitions. We are familiar with the research cited on Internet career sites, in business magazines and daily newspapers, and by career experts who blog, write, and proclaim the "news" that the best jobs are not advertised. In fact, networking is the number one, essential strategy mentioned for a successful search or career move, because, as *The Wall Street Journal* has reported, more than half of all jobs landed are found through personal contacts, referrals, and word of mouth—more than through advertisements, the Internet, and search firms combined. When we add these up, we realize that networking is a *must*, not a *maybe*. Have you ever looked at your career journey this way? Over the course of your work life, you will have worked *in*, worked *for*, and worked *with*; started, joined, led, left, returned, built, closed, and consulted. You will have created a portfolio of part-time, full-time, paid, and nonpaid work experiences. And it's very likely that you will have done none of this alone. Count up the people you've met and continue to meet along the way. Think about the opportunities and possibilities that can present themselves as you travel on your career journey, if you reach out to others not just during a job search, but every day, everywhere you find yourself.

Networking has big payoffs when we are comfortable with ourselves. When we are confident in our abilities to network we can increase our knowledge and gain leadership, team-building, and problem-solving skills. We can broaden our organizational effectiveness and get more things done, improve our business development efforts, and achieve our work-life goals. We can do all of this by seeking advice, receiving support, and tapping into others for their assistance (and for assistance from their networks) with our professional growth and advancement.

You may already be part of a great network. If you are, you know the value of being able to demonstrate your expertise, establish important relationships, and become known within and beyond your workplace or industry by offering help to others. You know it is not about the number of business cards and "links" you've collected, it's about the quality and variety of your network connections. It's not about title and rank, it's about trust and synergy. It's not about being a member of an exclusive club, but being part of a wide and diverse group that includes people of all ages, cultures, levels, backgrounds, skills, and interests. You have learned that networking is what connects people and moves careers forward!

SO, I ASK MYSELF:
WHY DON'T PEOPLE WANT TO NETWORK?

Just like the attendees at that long-ago breakfast who came in at the last minute to avoid making small talk or who sat beside someone they knew well, most people have a hundred reasons not to build a network. Over the years, I believe I've heard them all from clients and workshop participants. "It's not natural"; "I'm not good at it"; "It makes me uncomfortable to have to ask for help"; "I'm too shy." Some even say with great pride, "I'm too busy (to attend, join, take someone to lunch, etc.)." Other popular excuses are "What if they say no?" "I've never had to look for a job before." "I hate to beg." These are excuses, not reasons. The only authentic reason I've heard is "Networking means not being myself."

Over the past few decades, networking has justifiably developed a negative reputation. It's become known as "tell and sell," an unpleasant technique deployed during a job search, where its only purpose is to ask everyone you've ever known—or pretend you are interested in knowing—to give you "just one or two names." One of my clients called it "Hi, hire me" networking. No doubt you are familiar with the drill: compiling a long list of somewhat close, not so close, and never-met contacts, sending out a daily dose of e-mails, and then making unwanted and unsuccessful follow-up calls the next day. Like my clients, you have probably

Networking is a skill that can be learned.

spent money you did not have attending events, walking bravely into rooms crowded with strangers. You have dutifully stuck your name tag on the right-hand side of your jacket so that people can read it; you've skipped the refreshments so that you're free to shake hands with anyone reading that carefully placed name tag. Then you've "worked the room," hoping to hand out a dozen business cards or sit next to the head of "something," and tell people more about yourself than they would ever want to know. All in the hope that you'll run into, speak with, or meet one person who will say, "Come see me tomorrow about an opening."

Few situations create more anxiety than unemployment. I know. I've been there! During those stressful times, it seems the harder we try to network, the more difficult it becomes. Networking in the wake of a job loss or career move can make you feel lonely and phony, and concerned that some people may suspect your motives—especially if you have never offered to help them or asked for their help before. One can only imagine what a person thinks when a casual acquaintance boldly asks, "Would you submit my résumé to your HR department?" or "Will you pass my name up to your CEO?" or "Can I use your name to set up an informational meeting with your client?" Is this the way any of us really wants to network?

Networking doesn't work when you take people for granted and only try to connect with them when you need help. As Herminia Ibarra, professor of organizational behavior at INSEAD, the international business school with campuses in Europe and Asia, reminds us, "Most people are lousy at networking. They feel like they're trying to manipulate and put on a show. Networking is easier if you aren't thinking the whole time, 'Can this person get me a job?'" Truer words were never spoken. No wonder people are reluctant to network and they give it such a bad name.

And if you're thinking right now, "That's just the reason I don't attend networking events," remember that in the age of the Internet there is no escape. Who among us doesn't regularly receive e-mails from people we recently met or with whom we are barely acquainted, inviting us to just "click a button" and join their LinkedIn network or Facebook "friends" list?

In everyday networking, you bring a new attitude to bear on the whole process. For example, here's the old way of attending a breakfast meeting or conference event.

▷ Walk in to a crowded room with an attitude of dread, fear, or "What am I doing here?"

▷ Approach a dozen people with the goal of handing out your business card.

▷ Talk only about yourself.

Let's rethink and approach the same event in a new way.

▷ Go with the attitude of "What can I learn?" instead of "Who will I meet?"

▷ Do some advance research on the speaker, topic, and organization.

▷ Spend a few minutes at the registration desk and scan the name tags. Do you recognize a name or see someone from a company where you have a connection or whose product or service you are familiar with?

▷ Before walking into the room, find and introduce yourself to one of the board members or program committee members. Talk about why you are attending and ask if he knows of a particular attendee you should meet (or he could introduce you to).

▷ Circulate—don't "work the room!" Approach other attendees with a smile and with your hand extended to shake theirs, and introduce yourself (first and last names) with confidence. Read their name tags (or ask for their names), and then (here comes the part where you *learn*) . . .

▷ Before telling another attendee about yourself, ask a few questions that will begin a casual conversation. Why did she take time out of her day to hear this speaker? What are his professional interests? How long has he been a member of this group? What interesting activities is she involved in?

▷ And now, listen! Listen for information, for common interests, for an opportunity to introduce this person to other attendees who might share her background or interests. Networking with this learning attitude and "host" approach guarantees you will have an opportunity to make a connection or two and you will be seen as someone to know better.

Here's another new thought about networking. It doesn't happen only at "sanctioned" networking events. In fact, whether you are aware of it or not, you are always networking whenever you are in the company of another person. This reminds me of a story I read about "Eleanor," a marketing consultant. An important client invited her and several other professionals to watch a Boston Red Sox game from his skybox. During the game, the other guests lost no opportunities to schmooze the client, each outdoing the others in promoting his products and services. A long-time Sox fan, Eleanor joined her host's young son in enthusiastically cheering the home team. Her client had invited her to a game, and she concentrated on baseball, not business. She barely spoke to the client at all and awoke the next day concerned that she had "blown" a networking opportunity, so she was surprised and delighted when she received a large assignment from the client, who commented later that she and his son were the only people in the skybox who seemed to be having fun. By following the dictates of good manners and being courteous to her host and his family—in other words, by being authentic—Eleanor had networked more effectively than any of the others.

WHAT IS NETWORKING?

The spirit of networking as a way of life has probably been around as long as organized societies, but the term has been used to describe the business and career tool since the 1970s, when (not coincidentally) it started to be all about the outcome. We had the old boys' club, where deals were struck on golf courses or at the nineteenth hole. In the 1980s, networking became a buzzword synonymous with increasing sales and developing new business. With the coming of age of "Me, Inc." and "Free Agent" in the 1990s, networking became a science and the key to a successful job search. Millions of college graduates and outplaced senior executives learned the techniques. The "informational interview" and the sixty-second elevator pitch replaced exchanging ideas and connecting through real conversations.

Although many of these old-style activities continue today, we can bring networking full circle to realize its original intent: connecting authentically with a diverse group of people every day and creating endless opportunities for all concerned. In our careers and in our lives, networking puts us on a strong foundation of positive professional and personal interactions. It turns giving and receiving into activities we enjoy every day of our lives.

? Take minute or two and jot down your answers to the following questions.
  ▷ When you hear the word networking, what other words come to mind?
  ▷ What has been your best networking experience?
  ▷ Why do you network?
  ▷ What do your responses say about your networking attitude and approach?

The decision is yours: Is *networking* an overworked term that focuses only on external outcomes such as getting a job or receiving a promotion? Is *networking* all about putting on a façade, glad-handing, and keeping track of transactions so that you come out even in the end? If that's what *networking* means, let's drop the word from your career journey vocabulary—I'd like to drop it from the dictionary! Or does *networking* mean being yourself—your authentic self, a person who sees connecting with people as an integral work-life skill, something to do every single day? Once learned, the skill of networking can help you move in positive, purposeful directions over the long term.

More than anything else, everyday networking is *authentic* networking, and you will notice that I use both terms to describe the practices this book teaches. Only by behaving authentically can you bring networking to your everyday life. By bringing your best self to very encounter, you can rise above networking tips and tricks to take charge of your personal and professional lives, expand your view of the world, and reach new levels of accomplishment. Authentic networking promotes win-win situations; it brings people together in ways that make 1 plus 1 equal more than 2. It can change your life and make it better in ways you haven't even imagined.

WHAT IS AUTHENTIC NETWORKING?

I'm asking you to forget everything you have ever thought or been told about networking. Shift your mind from all the "I can'ts" we saw earlier in this chapter and all the transactional "how do I" techniques you've worried about mastering ("How do I meet him?" "How do I get my résumé in front of her?" "How do I leverage knowing you?"). Be open to the ideas and insights I have gleaned from more than twenty years working with clients and speaking to groups about networking as a job search and leadership tool. The first of those insights is this: The true purpose, value, and rewards of networking are discovered not at an event, on a golf course, or by reaching the corner office. Instead, we find them where the simple deeds and everyday actions of our lives offer small, significant opportunities to connect naturally with others and help us turn far-off dreams into achievable goals.

Authentic networking rests on these three principles.
▷ Networking is a skill that can be learned. It needs to be practiced, and then it becomes a habit, until finally it feels "natural."

▷ A network must be earned through thoughtful effort. Networks don't just happen.

▷ Networks are useful only when they serve their members. Networks are designed to be tapped, shared, and used.

Consider a simple, everyday example. Who likes finding or going to a new dentist? When you look for a new dentist, what do you do—besides procrastinate as long as that dull toothache allows? First you think about the kind of dentist you want and the locations and office hours that are convenient for you. Do you then call an 800 number for help? Or do you turn to your network of friends or colleagues for advice? Ten years ago, I found a new and fabulous dentist by calling Paula, a long-time friend who does due diligence better than anyone I know. An endorsement from Paula is as good as any hot stock tip I will ever receive. So, when she recommended Neil, I knew he would be a great dentist. Over the years, I, in turn, have recommended Neil to others, and some of those people have since recommended him to *their* colleagues. Through the power of a network, multiple referrals were made to one great dentist, all through—dare I say it?—word of mouth! Just as in your career, if you really need or want to do something in life, you find a way to do it. Having a network is one of the best ways to "do" almost anything.

Regardless of where we are in our career journeys, we can learn how to integrate networking into our daily lives. Once we stop relying on old-school techniques and tricks (such as calling before 8:00 a.m. or after 5:00 p.m. to "catch" the person instead of getting voice mail) and start focusing on why we are making the call and where to find the knowledge and experience connections we share, a new, real-world definition of networking begins to emerge. (And by the way, be wary of those so-called tricks! The reason that person is in the office early or late is to get organized or catch up on work. Your call may be an annoying intrusion.)

Authentic, everyday networking
▷ Reflects our core values and beliefs,
▷ Reinforces the laws of reciprocity,
▷ Promotes a spirit of generosity,
▷ Fosters awareness of our networking strengths,

▷ Acknowledges our anxieties (and awkwardness),

▷ Holds us accountable for our actions (and inactions),

▷ Helps us develop an honest assessment of our needs (versus our wants) and dreams,

▷ Allows us to articulate those needs and dreams in a clear and succinct message,

▷ And encourages us to listen to, accept, and appreciate the responses we receive.

When we redefine networking, we focus our attention and actions on becoming known as a person who is thoughtful, trustworthy, and sincere, a person who is genuinely interested in others—their professional needs and their personal interests. Authentic networking means we understand that great networks don't just happen and that networking isn't always "feel good" or predictable. Despite our discomfort, we make a long-term investment in time and energy to build relationships. We understand that reaching out to others may take courage, but that it is also about manners and common sense.

When we are authentic, we become more aware of who we are as people and what matters most to us; we build a work life that supports our efforts to be the best at what we do and to share our best with others. It is really quite simple and straightforward. Michelle Obama summed it up on the *Today Show* when Matt Lauer asked her what it was like to be first lady: "I approach this position like I approach my life. I try to be as authentically me as I can be because it's easier to maintain it. So, what people have seen over the course of the year is really Michelle. And I find a level of comfort in that role." Authentic networking can be one of our best career tools for achieving genuine success in work and everyday life because it opens our minds and it opens doors. It helps us shape a world full of people who enjoy taking our calls and who freely give us their time, sharing their ideas and answering our questions with honesty and good humor. We build a network of people who are as eager to help us as we are to help them.

You are always networking whenever you are in the company of another person.

You may be thinking, "This is easy for you to say, Patti; you've been networking for years and everyone knows you're an outgoing person. But networking doesn't come naturally to me." Ah, another excuse not to network. True, networking doesn't come naturally to most people. But being authentic is not the same as doing what comes naturally. Being authentic is being your own best self, reaching out to others in ways that are not always comfortable at first. It goes beyond our natural instincts and is a learned skill that improves with practice. But it's worth the effort.

WHY THIS BOOK?

Since that eye-opening breakfast meeting twenty years ago, I have spoken to thousands and coached hundreds of men and women in my role as a career and management consultant. I now want to pass along the valuable networking lessons I've learned firsthand and from my clients and colleagues.

My twenty-plus-year adventure has taken me to college campuses, corporate headquarters, coffee shops, and conference centers. It has given me an opportunity to work closely with a wide range of clients: recent college and MBA graduates, mid-career senior executives, onboarding professionals, and pre-retirees. Each of them was launching, building, restarting, or redirecting his or her work life. You will meet many of them in these pages. Some of the names have been changed and some of the details disguised, but the anecdotes spring from my life and work. Working with these individuals has allowed me to collect the best practices and principles of networking and to develop a lesson plan for a self-directed learning guide that will help you become the networker you want to be: an *authentic* networker—a person who can make a difference in the world and improve your own and other people's lives by building meaningful and lasting connections every day.

Networking opens the door to unlimited opportunities to give and to receive help.

THE SEVEN LESSONS

Networking is meant to build and strengthen reputations and relationships. It opens the door to unlimited opportunities to give and to receive help—

during a job search or career move, while building a business, or during any of life's personal adventures. It invites us to find ways to serve as a resource and to develop genuine rapport with the people we meet along our journeys. Through everyday networking, we learn that the greatest things are not achieved through luck, but by taking responsibility for our own attitudes and actions, and by being diligent in understanding and *exceeding* the needs and expectations of others.

Networking authentically makes the difference. Why? It requires us to successfully connect *who* we are with *what* we want and what we want to *do*. This real-world networking can be learned from seven simple, everyday life lessons. The first two lessons focus on your attitude, the next two on your approach, and the last three on the activities that support successful networking.

▷ **Lesson 1:** Take personal responsibility for managing your career and maintaining connections. Careers no longer "just happen" and networks don't fall into our laps; they must be earned.

▷ **Lesson 2:** Build a reputation you can be proud of, one you will want others to share with their own networks.

▷ **Lesson 3:** Develop genuine and long-lasting relationships. You will meet many people over the course of your working life. Get to know them and help them to know you, and your journey will be enriched in ways you never dreamed possible.

▷ **Lesson 4:** Establish rapport, not small talk. The strength of your network—bonds built on rapport—matters more than its size.

▷ **Lesson 5:** Master the basic requirements of networking. Learn and practice networking protocol and best practices by treating people and their time with respect.

▷ **Lesson 6:** Do your research. Gaining a solid understanding of someone's business and personal interests requires more effort than just looking him or her up on the Internet.

▷ **Lesson 7:** Reach out and become a valuable resource for others. Authentic networkers are reciprocators. For them, networking is an opportunity to give support and help whenever, wherever, and in whatever ways they can. They don't keep score.

START TODAY

Today is a great time to begin creating, expanding, and reaching out to your network. Each lesson in *The Power of Everyday Networking* will help you develop a networking process shaped by your own vision, attitude, personality, and values. Each lesson stands on its own and will direct your energy and efforts toward a more powerful and authentic approach to finding work, advancing in your career, or making a career change. Together, the seven lessons are landmarks you can visit and return to as you map out a personal networking strategy. They will guide you through the future and stand the test of time, no matter how employment conditions change or what professional and personal challenges you face. The seven lessons describe networking for the everyday world, in which the value of your network is based on the quality of the connections you've made, not the number of business cards you've collected or the social media sites you're on (although these are important tools). They will teach you how to network every day and for the long term.

Each of us wants to have a successful career journey. Are you ready to discover how you can succeed in work and in life? Why not begin today?

RESPONSIBILITY
It Starts and Ends with You

KATHLEEN APPROACHED ME after a Saturday morning networking workshop at an Ivy League career development event. Like many participants, she found my ideas about networking to be on target, and she agreed that a person must be himself or herself to build a lasting and meaningful network. Then came the "but I can't": "With a full-time job, kids, and a long commute, I don't have the time or energy to attend events or join a professional association, let alone take people out to lunch."

"Well," I replied, "do you have ninety minutes to meet me for lunch? Let's see how we can turn your *can't do* into a *can do*."

Two weeks later we met in a downtown restaurant known for letting its patrons converse in peace. I used the time before the food arrived to establish our rapport, then I asked: "Tell me, why did you make the time (on a Saturday no less) to attend my workshop?" She explained that she wanted to find a way to develop potential clients beyond the meet-and-greet activities most of her colleagues relied on. She wanted to expand her network to encompass a variety of professional women who would get together to exchange ideas that would help them all grow their businesses and their careers. Together we identified a number of business development networking options, all proven to "get results." But when I asked her when was she at her best making and building a real connection, I learned that what Kathleen enjoyed most was hosting large, casual dinner parties. Several times each year she invited a number of friends and acquaintances to spend time getting to know one another and learning about one another's work lives.

A year after our conversation, Kathleen had created a regional network of professional women from a cross section of industries, organizations, and institutions. These like-minded women meet for a few hours every few months and share the opportunity to listen to a well-known speaker, enjoy a glass of wine, hold conversations on anything and everything, and become part of a strong network of professional women. The concept was so innovative and successful that National Public Radio profiled it in a radio feature. And—most important—Kathleen was networking and reaping the rewards of increased visibility in a way that was enjoyable for her.

After graduating from a prestigious university, Ellen was disappointed when her applications to medical school were rejected. She had studied hard and gotten good grades in her pre-med courses, but one by one the thin envelopes of bad news arrived. Despondent, Ellen feared her dream of becoming a doctor would not come true and her hard work had been for nothing. Who was to blame—herself, or the "numbers game" of medical school admissions? And what should she do now?

Ellen thought she would make a good doctor, but she decided to test her commitment to the field of medicine. She applied for a job as a nurse's aide at a suburban hospital. Dealing with real patients every day would soon tell her if she was cut out for the realities of life as a physician. And if she decided to reapply, her year of working in a hospital setting would demonstrate how seriously she took her chosen career.

Ellen got the job and began caring for post-surgical patients, taking their vital signs and helping to feed and clean them. She became friendly with several patients over the course of their hospital stays. One morning, as Ellen went about her tasks with her usual calm and cheerful manner, a patient asked her about her background and her career aspirations. Ellen explained her situation, her failure to be accepted by a medical school, and her decision to test out her commitment to the field of medicine. Her patient surprised her by handing her his business card. "I haven't seen your transcript, but I am certain that you are exactly the kind of person that medicine needs today. Please send your application to my attention."

In Ellen's hand was the business card of the dean of a major Boston medical school—one that had rejected her application just months ago. She reapplied and was accepted the next year. Today she is a practicing physician.

✍

Once a successful and highly paid executive, Bob had "done everything right." He had gotten a good education, found a position in a growing company, worked hard, paid his dues, and stayed loyal. Still, when the company was acquired, he found himself "between opportunities," stumbling around in uncharted territory after years on the path to the corner office. Now, without a mentor to follow or a corporate ladder to climb, he wondered what to do next and which direction to take. Bob summed up the situation of many, if not most, people when he acknowledged to me, "So far, I have had an accidental career." He had sat by and let others decide the road he would take. He had let others take charge of managing and advancing his career for so long (and at first glance, so successfully) that at this important moment he wasn't even certain what he wanted to do next. And, unaccustomed to being in the driver's seat, he had a long list of concerns and doubts on how and whether he would be able to figure it out at this stage of his work life.

Bob did eventually take charge of his career transition. When he stopped relying on accident and luck, he was able to move beyond his doubts, explore his strengths, and define his areas of personal and professional interest.

✍

What's the lesson behind each of these stories? Responsibility is the foundation of success in everything you do. The levels of success and satisfaction that Kathleen, Ellen, and Bob achieved corresponded to their willingness and ability to take responsibility for their attitudes and actions.

TAKE RESPONSIBILITY FOR YOUR CAREER SUCCESS

Regardless of where you are in your career journey—from launching, like Ellen, to landing at a work-life crossroads, like Bob, or even deciding to finally write a book, like me—when you learn *why* and *how* to take personal responsibility for achieving work-life success and building the type of network you want, you take charge of what is happening in your life. You discover what matters most to you; you understand what motivates and interests you and what is important. Taking responsibility starts with understanding ourselves, finding and listening to the inner voice in each of us, and then deciding whether this voice will be a critic, preventing us from reaching our potential, or our greatest cheerleader, opening us up to the unlimited career and networking opportunities that each day brings.

What stops us from taking responsibility? We know all the reasons we should take charge, but, like Bob, we find it hard to give up the hope of having a successful "accidental career." *Wishful thinking* allows us to imagine the future without having to take charge of it. We *see* our success in one, three, or five years, imagining ourselves getting a promotion, landing a major client, appearing on the *New York Times* bestseller list, or starting our own business, but we don't act on the vision. Oh, we weave our goals and dreams into our networking and workday conversations. We may even recognize that it will take extra time and a lot of work, and we may actually believe we are up to the challenge. But then, instead of identifying the sense of achievement that comes from making something happen and then taking action to reinforce it, we focus on our self-doubt ("Can I really do this?" "Is this really worth the effort?") and indecision ("Is this the right time?" "How will I find the time?"). We worry about the risks ("Can I afford to do this?") and fear the what-ifs ("What if no one reads my book; or worse, what if they do and hate it?"). Or we procrastinate and make excuses ("When I have more . . ." or "Once I'm free to . . ."). Each of us can go through our own exercise of self-analysis and list the reasons we think we won't attain success (you may want to do that now in your notebook).

Responsibility is the foundation of success in everything you do.

We all have attitudes that inhibit us from choosing what we wish to do; other attitudes keep us tied to what we wish not to do. But identifying the negative attitudes that misdirect us from our professional and personal priorities is only the first step. Having done that, can we find the way—do we take responsibility—to reach our dreams and goals?

Management expert and author Peter Drucker once noted, "Successful careers are not planned. They develop when people are prepared for opportunities because they know their strengths, their method of work, and their values." Drucker emphasized the importance of knowing your own values and gifts in finding direction: "Most people, especially highly gifted people, do not really know where they belong until they are well past their mid-twenties. By that time, however, they should know the answers to three questions: What are my strengths? How do I perform? And What are my values? And then they can and should decide where they belong—or where they do *not* belong."

Determining what we value and preparing ourselves for opportunities requires us to occasionally stop, step back, and engage in an internal dialogue. What are your values? For some people, family is foremost. For others, personal integrity is the most important value. What are your highest strengths? Fashion industry veteran Julie Mannion describes one of her strengths as "the ability to see the big picture and work backwards from that." Your strengths may be your analytical skills, your flexibility, or your creativity.

Author David Maister, a management consultant and former Harvard Business School professor, says, "Success comes from doing what you enjoy. If you don't enjoy it, how can it be success?" What do you enjoy, and how can you integrate it into your networking approach and activities? When we start taking responsibility for our career and networks, we are becoming authentic, knowing who we really are. We recognize that our attitude—not our ability—controls whether and how much we enjoy the journey. But don't make the mistake of taking responsibility for your career or networking *only* in times of obvious or painful change. Take responsibility every day, and your course will become clearer and lead to more interesting places with fewer dead ends. And your network of traveling companions will make the journey more enjoyable.

SHORT-TERM THINKING

When Bob, the "accidental" executive, found himself at a career standstill, he wishfully looked back at the easy successes of his early career. Wishful thinking is just one example of short-term, transactional thinking, an attitude of expecting immediate benefits from any effort: "If I do this, he will do that, and this will happen." This kind of thinking undermines our success, yet is very common when we are going through the dozens of transitions we face over the course of our work life. Consider the most frequent example: a job search. Richard was about to graduate from an MBA program and was considering a job offer. When I asked him what he liked about the job, he excitedly told me about the size of the firm, his title, opportunities to travel, how many people he would manage, his starting salary, and related benefits—all short-term thinking based on external measurements and focused on external rewards. Once Richard took a breath, I asked him some longer-term questions: What will you learn? Can and will you make an impact or contribution in the first twelve months? Who and how many different departments in the organization will you work with? What's your understanding of the company culture and work ethics? What will you give up by taking this position over another? Where will this position take you next? And then where? My final question was: "Richard, when the job is over, what will you be known for?"

Everyday, authentic networking doesn't always have immediate tangible results. This gets people down if their thinking is short-term, or if they expect immediate payoffs for every networking effort. Many clients have told me in frustration, "Well, I met with so-and-so and nothing happened." Or "That meeting was worthless." But was it? When I hear that a meeting was "worthless," I suggest that the client think back to the meeting: Did the other person give you an idea? Did she confirm something? Did she give you a new perspective or a different point of view? Did the person feel the meeting was worth *her* time and energy?

And then I ask: How did you take responsibility for making this a successful meeting? Were your intentions and expectations for holding the meeting clear and realistic? Too often we go into a meeting with our primary goal or expectation being a job lead or an introduction to someone in the other person's network. A more long-term, authentic intention would be to think of it as an opportunity to meet someone who is giving you his or her time—probably the scarcest resource around today—to get to know you, to develop a stronger relationship, and to decide if and how he may want to help you (and how you can help him). This long-term takeaway can be more valuable than a couple of random names gleaned from a forty-five-minute meeting. Or perhaps that initial meeting was just a necessary prelude to a more productive one to come.

I also want to know: Did you come prepared with extra copies of your résumé or with real-world stories that demonstrate your strengths, values, and transferable skills? Were your questions mindful of this person's responsibilities and work pressures—about *his* industry's future, *his* business challenges and *his* career journey? Did you have something to offer—that is, did you bring either knowledge or insight to the table that would turn your networking meeting into a "meeting of the minds"?

"Worthless" meetings, based on short-term thinking, try to "tell and sell." When we rethink networking meetings and base them on long-term thinking, we establish rapport and create opportunities to listen and learn. So, stop thinking short-term and let your attitude and networking agenda mirror your career and life—both long-term propositions. Remember the case of Ellen—now Dr. Ellen? Ellen wasn't "networking" as she took her patient's temperature. She was simply doing a good job while making each personal encounter of her day, her week, her month, her year as a nurse's aide as positive and pleasant as possible. She wasn't going to judge her success by what happened on a particular day. Ellen had a long-term view.

A long-term perspective will carry you through obstacles that would stop short-term thinkers in their tracks. With an attitude of being open, interested, and curious, viewing every interaction and every mistake as an opportunity to learn, you broaden the meaning and possibilities of networking.

That's why the first lesson authentic networkers learn is the importance of taking *responsibility* for their career, their behavior, and their community. Responsibility means creating a personal definition of career success that is driven by one's own attitude and personality. It means being open to a journey full of new experiences and transitions where opportunities lead to professional and personal development and growth.

BE RESPONSIBLE FOR YOUR NETWORK

People sometimes ask me, "How can I be authentic and network?" Here's an answer that might change your attitude: How can you network if you are *not* authentic? The responsibility for getting connected and developing an authentic approach to networking success begins and ends with you. That responsibility cannot be delegated. It depends entirely on you.

Remember the three principles of networking authentically. One, networking is a lifetime skill. It can be learned, and the process becomes natural with practice over time. Two, networks are all about relationships, and they must be earned. Through long-term effort and good intentions, you will develop connections with the people you meet along the way and take these relationships with you over your

A long-term perspective will carry you through obstacles that would stop short-term thinkers in their tracks.

career. And three, a network is most effective when it works to benefit you and the members of your network. In short, approach networking with an attitude of "How can I help?" and not "Here's what I do."

Every day, with every personal and professional action you take, you are networking. Building and tending your network is less an activity than an attitude and an approach to how you operate. It's not a project to be accomplished, but an ongoing part of your life. So, in addition to evaluating your career from time to time, give equal attention to your network. Why is your network the size it is? Why doesn't it have more—or fewer—members? Why are these people in it and not others? How often do you talk with the people in your network? Is your network diverse and evolving or stagnant and out of date? What steps are you taking to connect your network with the networks of others? You can't create a network and then file it away on a contact list and forget about it. If you don't engage it regularly, it becomes a worthless relic of past contacts, old acquaintances, and bygone times. Only regular use will keep it alive and vital.

You must also support your network by giving more than you get. Author Deiric McCann reminds us that the best networkers "give their ideas, referrals, contact support, expertise, enthusiasm, energy, time, humor, and anything else they reasonably can. Even before they've won anything of value from a new acquaintance." You may feel you don't have a lot to offer at this time, but you will be amazed how much value you can create just by linking people you know to others who can benefit from getting acquainted and having an opportunity to exchange ideas and share knowledge.

My friend Madelyn is a natural at doing this; she has an amazing ability to "put people together." I'm writing this section after just having attended an event she called "Women You Need to Know." Madelyn and her network connection, Carolyn, went with their instincts and sent out a spur-of-the-moment e-invite to twenty women to meet at a local restaurant. Madelyn and Carolyn knew people who would enjoy knowing one another, so they took action, put it together, and were open to seeing what would happen. Guess what! With no fuss and no muss, sixteen women showed up and had a great time. Several discovered they were in the same industry and had mutual connections. Some exchanged business cards. All of them had a great evening. Two days later, Madelyn followed up with an e-mail containing each attendee's name, e-mail address, and Web site. She did this because she wanted to, not because she had to. That's taking responsibility for your network!

BECOME AWARE OF YOUR ATTITUDE AND ACTIONS

Years ago, I heard a very senior executive answer the question "Why have you been so successful?" with this response: "We all know that old phrase, '80 percent of success is showing up.' Well, I showed up." Everyone laughed, and then he went on to say, "I showed up with an attitude ready, willing, and wanting to be my best, do my best, and give my best." That executive's response made me realize our attitude defines where we focus our attention and how we look ahead to the future. Coaches tell their teams, "Attitude is a decision." Our attitude determines the career direction we want to take and how we respond to what life brings us and asks of us. From the perspective of authentic networking, attitude shapes our approach and our actions every day; and it is directly related to how we relate to others. All of these things affect our career success.

Maybe you're thinking "OK, I get it," and you feel you have a "good" or "positive" attitude. Like that senior executive, you "show up," you do your job, and you try to stay upbeat and cheerful during times of transition. You understand the importance of helping others and know the benefits of building relationships in both the real and online worlds. So, what's missing? The other 20 percent: showing up with an *open* attitude—that is, an attitude that opens you up to the unexpected, whether you call it luck, coincidence, chance, or serendipity; being willing to try something new and step out of your comfort zone by responding positively, professionally, and practically—instead of complaining about what can't happen or reacting emotionally to what did happen; acknowledging shortcomings, welcoming honest feedback, and taking full responsibility for your mistakes.

Stuart, a client, taught me a great work-life lesson about this when he said, "I used to think of my mistakes as failures; now I see them as reference points." Now, that is an open attitude! Being open means being able to reduce or replace anxieties about the potential obstacles and pitfalls of networking with an attitude of "You win some, you lose some." Thomas Edison is widely reported to have said, "I have not failed 1,000 times. I have successfully discovered 1,000 ways to *not* make a light bulb." Or in the words of the old song that, once heard, lingers in your head: "Pick yourself up, dust yourself off, start all over again."

How Open Is Your Attitude?

No matter what the topic, your attitude can be open or it can be closed. When your attitude is open, you are willing to question and learn more about a subject.

? To find out if you have an open attitude toward networking, jot down the thoughts, feelings, and phrases that come to mind when the following events happen to you.
  ▷ You are invited to attend an event where you know other attendees.
  ▷ You are invited to an event where you don't know other attendees.
  ▷ You need to call someone you barely know or you need to ask a friend for a favor.
  ▷ Someone asks you for a "quick" favor when your time is limited.

The language of your responses can expose some of your underlying attitudes. Do your answers say "My mind is open to the possibilities of what I can do," or do they say "My mind is focused on what I can't do"? Phrases such as "Ugh, another night out" or "I've heard that topic before; the speaker won't say anything new" or "It's not in my nature to . . ." or "I feel so awkward when . . ." expose attitudes of *won't do, can't do,* indifference, fear, or helplessness. Do you avoid accountability by saying "If only my industry hadn't collapsed" or "If only I were twenty years younger" or "If only the best medical schools weren't so exclusive"?

You can reduce your networking anxieties and make them more manageable by reframing your thoughts, saying, "I am learning how to . . ." instead of "I feel so powerless when . . ."; "I like to prepare well before I call strangers," instead of "I'm afraid to call strangers on the phone"; "This is interesting, let's see what happens," instead of "There is no way I'm going to do that!"

Over the next few days, observe and acknowledge the number of times your attitude leads to *can't*, *won't*, or *don't* words or phrases and start replacing them with *might*, *maybe*, or *I'm willing to think about it* language. This simple and proactive way of taking responsibility will help you harness the power of networking. Remember, a "can't do" attitude will defeat you before you take the first step. A "can do" attitude will help you and your networking and move your career in the right direction. How can you make the adjustment to *can* from *can't*? Here's a hint from Henry Ford: "If you think you can do a thing or think you can't do a thing, you're right."

TAKE RESPONSIBILITY FOR THOUGHTS THAT SPRING FROM YOUR ATTITUDES

OK, you are going to take responsibility for managing your career, and you will adjust your attitude and work on being more open in your choice of words and daily networking deeds. But what about those thoughts that just seem to pop into your mind whenever you get ready to make that initial phone call or sign up to attend an event for the first time or, worse, attend alone?

Your thoughts are powerful and often contradictory. They are your responses to the "What might happen?" questions. Your thoughts can give you the confidence to be comfortable with who you are, making you willing to step out into the unknown. Your thoughts can also intimidate you so much that you resist trying things you really want to do. They can make you defensive or embarrassed and build walls of doubt and fear around you. Fear puts you off balance. It creates stress, tension, and a feeling of powerlessness. It turns inner calm into uncertainty and is the primary reason most of us don't achieve our dreams and goals. What are you afraid of? What keeps you from networking in a way that feels true to yourself and authentic to others?

The best way to deal with fear isn't to suppress it or pretend it's not there. It's to acknowledge it. Examine your fears head-on: Study them and put each in its proper place. By examining the thoughts that hold you back you can determine if your fears are reasonable and take practical steps to mitigate them. For example, for some people, standing up and asking a question of the speaker at a professional association meeting can arouse anxiety and negative thoughts. Will the question be on target? Will my voice be clear and my question audible, or will I be asked to "speak up" or repeat my question? These are reasonable concerns, but they can be addressed by preparing a question carefully (even writing it out) and speaking loudly. Fear can also stop us from expressing a new idea or voicing an unpopular opinion at a staff meeting. A practical antidote to this fear is to spend some time learning about the meeting's likely topics of conversation and doing research to back up your idea or point of view.

Maybe you are one of those people who will never ask a question in a public meeting or conference session. Maybe you are shy or introverted and fear standing around and making small talk with others. Shyness is real and part of all of us. But rather than dreading speaking with others, put shyness to work for you by asking questions and letting others do most of the talking. Always remember: Don't be afraid of the thing or activity you fear—be afraid instead of letting fear prevent you from acting. The paralysis caused by fear is what Franklin D. Roosevelt referred to during the Great Depression when he said, "The only thing we have to fear is fear itself."

Fear of Rejection

Networking involves risk, which can cause you to avoid taking action. All fears constrain us, but the biggest barrier to authentic networking is the fear of rejection. No one likes rejection, and most people will go to great lengths to avoid situations where rejection is a possibility. Sometimes people are so concerned about getting turned down that they don't even ask. But to be a successful networker, you have to stretch yourself beyond your comfort zone—which means risking rejection. Consider the case of author Paul

Harding. His novel was rejected so many times that he almost resigned himself to being an unpublished writer. But he persisted and did not allow rejection to deter him. Finally he found a publisher through a referral from one of the editors who had turned his manuscript down. His book, *Tinkers*, won the 2010 Pulitzer Prize.

Fear will never go away, and rejection happens to everyone, every day. So what? It's not the worst thing that can happen. Rethink your approach and adopt the attitude that most people in the world welcome sincere interaction. You may still have momentary anxiety about asking a person you don't know to meet for coffee, but you will follow that up by asking yourself, "What's the worst thing that could happen if she says no or I feel like she's brushing me off?" Answer: "We won't have coffee that day." An even better answer: "I'll call someone else to meet for coffee instead."

Few times are more stressful than when you are looking for work, making you extra-sensitive to rejection. You may take rejection very personally, or avoid asking for anything because you are embarrassed that you need help. Maybe you avoid calling a person because the last time you spoke she cut you off after only a few *Approach networking with an attitude of "How can I help?"* minutes. Stop a moment and think about what might be going on in her life. Especially if you are in a period of transition, it is easy to focus on your own wants and needs and to miss seeing what's going on with others. Drop this "it's-all-about-me" mindset and recognize that other people may be preoccupied or have worries you don't know about. Everyday networking is a discovery process. Part of that process is discovering how your skills, interests, and experience can be of value to others and then developing a network where you can share them. Another part of the discovery process is acknowledging the networking activities you can't imagine doing and not doing them—*yet*!

TAKE RESPONSIBILITY FOR YOUR BEHAVIORS

Attitudes and thoughts produce behaviors which, when repeated enough, become habits. Habits are, in fact, learned behaviors, so any habit can be changed. As you did with your thoughts, start with an honest assessment.

Acknowledge and address behaviors that have become habits that are counterproductive to developing relationships and that don't meet the requirements for building a network. Negative behaviors fall into several categories. Do you have a habit of not returning phone calls in a timely manner? That can show a lack of courtesy. When you agree to meet someone for lunch or after work, do you chronically arrive even a

"I used to think of my mistakes as failures; now I see them as reference points."

few minutes late? That can be seen as uncaring and rude. A common habit is interrupting others, wanting to get out your story. People may see you as someone who just "has to have the floor" or who doesn't know how to listen. Do you procrastinate and frequently need to apologize for not following through? Or do you find yourself frequently explaining your actions—or inaction? We can all identify ourselves occasionally behaving in some or all of these ways. It's when these habits are seen as part of your modus operandi that they stand between you and your goals.

Making excuses is one of the least productive behaviors you can indulge in. Fears easily turn into excuses such as "I've never been good at that," or "It's too much to ask." Convincing yourself that you can't change your old habits is simply an excuse for not trying.

Excuses can team up with procrastination, telling you that you're just not ready to start; or you really don't have the time today; or you just have to get some materials, phone numbers, and names ready. Maybe you're waiting for the perfect time or for more information. Recognize these common procrastination traps and learn to tell the difference between taking a legitimate (and brief) pause to get a different perspective and procrastinating in order to avoid possible failure or rejection. Taking responsibility for your behaviors means managing your excuses by putting each one to the truth test. Is there *really* no time to make that call before lunch?

Fortunately, habits can be "unlearned" too. Research tells us it takes twenty-one days to make or break a habit. That means if you perform your desired activity—flossing your teeth, going to the gym, or saying "please" and "thank you"—for twenty-one consecutive days, you will have created a new habit, hopefully a better one. For instance, a person with a habit of making self-serving excuses ("I really don't have time to call anyone in my network") can, with practice, develop the opposite habit of accountability. A person who is accountable always takes responsibility for his or her behavior and for what he or she does or fails to do. A reputation for accountability, in turn, earns the trust and confidence of others. The notion of accountability starts with being accountable to oneself: for moving forward, for building a supportive network, for accomplishing goals.

What behaviors and habits are impeding your progress? Make a list of them and then indicate the habits you will cultivate in their stead, as in the following table.

Bad Habits	*Desired Behaviors*
Lack of courtesy	Everyone deserves to be treated with courtesy and respect. As my sister told her son, if you can't think of anything nice to say, try harder.
Procrastination	Deliver assignments or promised actions on time. Create artificial deadlines: If something is due Tuesday, I set a Monday deadline. It buys me time when I need it.
Tardiness	Train yourself to arrive a few minutes early.
Interrupting others	Count to ten silently to allow others to have their say before interjecting your view.
Failing to reciprocate	Practice giving first and giving without expecting anything in return.

TAKE RESPONSIBILITY FOR GIVING BACK

Tony Bennett's success as a singer spans four decades. He is also a fine painter, a businessman, and a person who has always made it his practice to give back. In a recent interview he said, "You can hit it big in America, make lots of money and have lots of success. But if you do it without integrity, that is a very empty experience. My advice to anyone who has been fortunate to be successful is to take, but make sure you give back as well."

Volunteering may be the greatest win-win work-life experience you can have during your career. Make it a part of your networking activities as soon as you can, because volunteering teaches you the value of helping others and the lessons of stewardship and service. Volunteering can be a powerful way to get to know the community and to be known in the community. Your choice of volunteer opportunity—civic organization, political group, church or religious organization, charity, or museum—may depend on where you want to focus. Some activities will support your personal interests, while others, such as lending a hand at your industry professional association, will help you in your career. Other volunteer efforts can foster your leadership abilities. All volunteer activities will introduce you to a variety of people and give you the chance to make lasting relationships.

Before joining any volunteer organization, you need to consider where you can contribute most. Participating in the group's activities lets you see where your talents and skills are most valued; it lets you sharpen your leadership skills without having formal authority. You can discover new and fulfilling activities or expand your business acumen, learning in an environment where each action is done for the greater good. For example, if cold-calling leaves you cold, volunteer for a school or charity telethon and you will quickly learn to sharpen your communication, sales, and persuasion skills by spending a few hours "dialing for dollars" for your favorite cause. Make volunteering a part of your lifestyle, not because you think you can get business out of it or it boosts your career advancement, but as a way to build and gain the respect and trust of others—two of the most valued gifts any networker can receive. Finally, giving selflessly to others helps each of us appreciate how fortunate we are, even when times seem difficult, which boosts our confidence and self-esteem.

Authentic networking is a discovery process.

We all have plenty of job, family, and other obligations, so finding the time for volunteer work can be challenging. But no matter how busy you think you are, there is always time to give back. As Fran Gallitano, a dear friend and amazingly giving woman, told me, "Some days, you just give back more than others." Many of the world's busiest people find the time to give back to their communities; Bill Gates and Warren Buffett are just two of many famous examples. Like them, be smart about how, when, and where you volunteer. Be realistic about your time commitments by choosing just one civic or charitable organization. Start slowly. Participate at a specific event or as a guest before becoming an active member. Over time, and if it's working for you, make this activity a part of your life. Remember, you are volunteering: Do it because you want to, not because you feel like you have to or you think it will be useful.

BECOME RESPONSIBLE FOR YOUR RELATIONSHIPS

Remember one of our authentic networking principles: A network must be earned. A network is made up of people, and its success is built on the strength of the relationships with *each* individual. It's your responsibility to establish, support, and maintain these relationships. As John, a consummate networker, likes to remind me: "My jobs may end, but my relationships don't end; they just change." Building and nurturing relationships takes time—for phone calls, meetings over coffee, and lunch dates. It takes energy—for planning, attending, and following up. And it takes effort—for writing thank-you notes, e-mailing newsworthy information, and giving for no reason at all. Think of these as daily investments, small but important networking steps. Retired GE CEO Jack Welch underscored the value of networking and interpersonal skills while speaking to students at MIT's Sloan School of Management in 2005. When a participant asked, "What should we be learning in business school?" Welch replied, "Just concentrate on networking. Everything else you need to know, you can learn on the job."

Like Ellen and Bob, even the most successful professionals will confess that their careers have been guided to some extent by circumstances, chance, good luck, or influential people. Have you had a similar experience? School guidance counselors, campus recruiters, mentors, or headhunters may have played prominent roles in your choices. But while others may influence the direction of your life and career, only one person is ultimately responsible for its success: you! Not your boss, your spouse, or your parents. It's you, and it is up to you to follow your passion in work and in life so that you can enjoy and take pride in both. The alternative to personal responsibility is the "accidental" career and life that so many experience. Redefining networking and learning to become an everyday networker allow you to approach your life and build your network with the attitudes, thoughts, and

Volunteering may be the greatest win-win work-life experience you can have.

behaviors that recognize that no one travels the career journey alone. Knowing that, it is important to acknowledge the help you receive and seek out opportunities to help others every day.

Questions for Reflection

▷ Have you had an accidental career? How can you begin to take more personal responsibility for how your career moves forward?

▷ Do you know your strengths and your values? Are they aligned with what you are doing in your current work life?

▷ What are some of the everyday ways you network? What are some of your excuses for not networking?

▷ What have you recently accomplished in spite of your fear?

▷ What volunteer activities do you pursue? Why? How do they benefit you and the community they serve?

REPUTATION
Making a Name for Yourself

A FORMER CLIENT CALLED not long ago to say he had given my name to a friend. When he mentioned his friend's name, my immediate response was, "Wait a minute—isn't that the fellow who started up the company that just had a huge IPO? What does he need *my* help for?" The man who launched the company; the woman who turned the hospital around; the team that developed the innovation; the person who invented . . .

If your name came up in conversation, what would people say about you? After they had met you, what would they say to others? What we're talking about is your reputation. Reputation determines how much people trust or mistrust you and how much they want to be part of your network and networking efforts. Your reputation distinguishes you and provides a value that goes beyond impressive titles and material trappings.

This lesson explores the importance of developing a positive reputation; it explains why you must never take your reputation for granted or leave it to chance. Throughout your personal and professional life, you must always be building it, maintaining it, and protecting it. Your reputation is an intangible asset and will be the most significant factor in developing and keeping your network. In studying reputation, you will see how word of mouth conveys information about performance and behavior to the world at large, helping people form judgments about people they haven't yet met.

Reputation affects how we are perceived from the first encounter with others and often sets the tone of our relationships. In the long run, it's less about credentials and more about credibility, competence, and confidence. We have all met someone and exclaimed, "I've heard so much about you!" Or, when asked if we know so-and-so, we've answered, "Only by reputation."

WHAT'S IN A NAME?

Some years ago, I was active in a human resources professional association. One day I was seated in the back row of a seminar offered by the group. It started with the customary introductions of the attendees. In the front row, a new member who was also new to the field stood and introduced herself: "Hi, my name is Patricia Hunt." She gave a brief overview of her background and then sat down. Several people turned around and gave me a look. Five rows and ten minutes later, I stood and, mimicking the classic television show "To Tell the Truth," said, "Hi, *my* name is Patricia Hunt."

Many in the room smiled, because they had known and worked with me for years. Same name, same professional interests, attending the same professional association meeting, in the same room, yet two different people with different experiences and different histories and, therefore, different reputations.

Reputation encapsulates everything about you. It is the earned outcome of your actions, background, education, experiences, credentials, and competencies. It is determined and continuously shaped by your achievements, professional affiliations, activities, and personal guiding values and principles. Reputation is never "finished"—it's always "in the making," being enhanced or diminished. Just as you are always networking, you are always building up or tearing down your reputation.

In a professional world, reputation is an invisible but important part of your résumé. While the printed page includes titles you have held and successes you have achieved, your "living" reputation—via the grapevine or your references—will answer the truly relevant questions: Are you a self-starter? Are you a problem-solver? Can you think on your feet? Will you fit in? Are you trustworthy? Do you have integrity?

Reputation is a snapshot of our character, commitments, and achievements, defining us to the world. For better or for worse, we become "the person who brought out the best in everyone," or ". . . led the team to success," or ". . . caused others to politely decline when they heard he was attending." Consider the case of Chesley B. "Sully" Sullenberger, the pilot who safely landed a crippled airliner on the Hudson River in January 2009. Sullenberger was already well known within his industry, but few outside the airline world knew anything about him. Yet his deeds on that day earned him a reputation throughout the United States for steadiness and professionalism under pressure—as a person anyone could count on in a tight situation, and the guy we would be happy to see at the controls of whatever airplane we were traveling on.

Your reputation is an intangible asset.

? Take a moment now to jot down the elements of your reputation, and then describe how you wish your life and career would be thought of by others. How do they compare? Which elements of your reputation fall short of the ones you'd like to be known for?

Reputation is important in developing and sustaining a network. As baseball Hall of Famer Ted Williams famously said, "Your reputation reaches people before you do." Before a person has had a chance to meet you in person, he or she may have formed a personal judgment about you because your reputation has preceded you. This judgment may just be a first impression— but we all know how strong first impressions are.

Reputation travels fast and, fairly or unfairly, once it arrives, it is hard to shake. Once it's established, it is what people are most likely to remember about you, and not simply because it sums up who you are, what you stand for, and the company you keep. The main reason it is so memorable is that a reputation often carries emotional information. It's not just what people know about you, it's how they *feel* about what they know. People communicate this feeling every time they mention you; it is expressed by the tone of a voice or the arch of an eyebrow.

A positive reputation is your most important career and networking asset. It's what differentiates you from the other people in their network. And it lingers. The late Ann Richards, governor of Texas from 1991 to 1995, had a charismatic personality and many accomplishments to her credit. When she

33

lost the governorship to G.W. Bush, she was confident that her reputation was strong: "I think I am leaving with a tremendous amount of goodwill on the part of the people of Texas." Do you have this much confidence in your reputation?

HOW IS A REPUTATION BUILT?

Your professional reputation is founded on four elements. First, you are known and judged by the profession you have chosen. Every field has reputational cachet and liabilities. While the key to career happiness may be doing what you love, it is important to consider what others think of the work you have chosen. What do you think of when you read these words: *teacher; banker; engineer; doctor; lawyer; plumber; writer*?

A profession's reputation is based on several factors. Is the profession growing or in decline? Are its products or services innovative, competitive, and in demand? Is the profession seen as client-focused, helpful to others, or self-interested? Is it harming consumers or the planet? As with individuals, professions—for many reasons—go through tough times and can acquire negative reputations. Events in the news over the past decade have caused the public reputations of accounting firms, Wall Street bankers, and even some well-known charitable organizations to plummet. And fair or not, the good names of people with years of honest and hard work to their credit suffer the consequences when their professions fall into disrepute.

The second element of reputation is the organization you work for and therefore represent. What is its history—is it a start-up, a family-owned business, or a Fortune 500 company? What have been its significant events—innovative new-product introductions, reorganizations, messy management changes? As long as you and your name are associated with it, you will either feel pride in the organization you work for or need to apologize for it. Henry was proud of his twenty years of contributions and growth at major firms. That ended when his last employer was acquired by a firm whose name was synonymous with scandal—whose executives were seen in the courtroom as much as in the boardroom.

Is your organization known for the highest quality and integrity? Is it seen as innovative or as a stodgy corporate fossil? Is leadership based on a management hierarchy or is it seen as flexible and entrepreneurial? These public impressions become part of your reputation; they speak to culture, work style, and motivation. Think of the difference between the stereotypes of Google employees—nonstop, hard-working, creative, and inspired—and employees of less highly regarded companies. And pity the thousands of conscientious government employees whose reputations are at the mercy of a few very public bad apples.

Professional, real-world experience makes up the third component of reputation. This is where your functional expertise, your achievements, and your accomplishments define you. Within your firm, your reputa-

A positive reputation is your most important career and networking asset.

tion is based on your résumé, roles, and responsibilities, as well as with the workplace "sound bites" you have earned along the way: *team player*; *decision maker*; *straight shooter*; *has your back*. (I will leave it to you to jot down whatever negative sound bites come to your mind.)

Your professional reputation is also formed by how you engage and work with external contacts. Clients, suppliers, competitors, and members of your professional community all form opinions of you by the way you do your job, respect their time and efforts, and conduct business with them.

The final building block of your reputation is your own character. It is the part you should focus on and care most about. You may not be able to control the events that affect the reputations of your profession, the company you work for, or even the role you play within it, but who you are and the qualities of character you bring to the world *are* within your control. They can be summed up in a single acronym: ETHICS.

ETHICS: THE AUTHENTIC "YOU"

ETHICS stands for Expertise, Trust, Honesty, Integrity, Creativity, and Stewardship. Your expression of these qualities represents your core personal values and beliefs. These are as deep-seated and unchanging as your DNA. They contribute enormously to your personal reputation, which is the single greatest influence in the success of your career and networking efforts.

Expertise sums up what you know, what you are good at, and what you are known for. Expertise is more than the accomplishments listed in your résumé or LinkedIn profile; in fact, it may not even be spelled out on your résumé in so many words. Instead, it is a talent, a "knack," or a skill that transcends and supports your achievements. Perhaps it's your ability to get conflicting parties to come together to solve problems, or your "sixth sense" about new-product opportunities. Maybe you succeed where others have failed, leaving your company in better shape than it was before you arrived. Let's hope that your expertise is positive, that you are known as a problem-solver and not as a problem!

The next three letters in ETHICS stand for words that describe what you are as a person and define how you deliver your expertise to the world. *Trust* determines the degree to which people want to work with or for you; it supports your ability to be influential beyond the reaches of your formal authority. Do people trust you? Are you considered reliable? Consistent? Fair? Do you keep the confidences of others as carefully as you keep your own? Lack of trust undermines relationships and tarnishes reputations, slamming and permanently closing doors that would otherwise be open.

> *Genuine curiosity about people is fundamental to authentic networking.*

Honesty, while related to trustworthiness, means more than just telling the truth. It means you recognize and acknowledge your limits. When you are honest about what you can and can't do, you free yourself from impossible expectations that will only disappoint you and others. With this kind of truthfulness, you establish credibility.

Sharing your expertise with *Integrity* means keeping your word. You honor your promises, both explicit and implicit. You play fair and achieve success without underhanded tricks or dubious shortcuts. Warren Buffet once said that he looks for three qualities in any partner or employee: energy, intelligence, and integrity. The first two traits, he added, are dangerous without the third.

Creativity reflects how you view the world. A creative person is always building, not tearing down; she focuses on the future and is not stuck in the past. A creative person shares ideas and suggestions. Creativity is closely connected with the quality of curiosity; a creative person sees himself as a student and is continuously learning about ideas, things, and people. Genuine curiosity about people—their dreams, their interests, their lives—is fundamental to authentic networking.

Finally, your reputation includes information on how you give back to society, your *Stewardship* or service orientation. Stewardship encompasses more than being active in your community or volunteering, although as we learned in the previous lesson those are important. Remember that reputation is as much about how people feel about you as it is about the facts. People know whether you have a generous spirit and willingly give back as much as or more than you get, whether you share useful information or hoard it for your own benefit. Stewardship is based on an attitude of service, an attitude that reaches beyond volunteer activities to look at events from another person's point of view. It starts with the question "How can I help?" and not with "Here's what I do." It ends by becoming a resource to others—sharing time, assistance, and knowledge freely.

? What are your ETHICS?

  ▷ What Expertise are you known for? (can be more than one)

  ▷ Have you established a reputation for Trust? How or how not?

  ▷ Are you Honest about your strengths and weaknesses, acknowledging them to yourself and others?

  ▷ Are you known for Integrity? Do you always deliver what you promise?

  ▷ Would people describe you as Creative? Why or why not? What creative activities do you pursue outside work?

  ▷ How have you demonstrated Stewardship?

THE REALITIES OF REPUTATION

Your reputation is a work in progress. Every day, your actions and behaviors add to or detract from it. And beyond your actual actions, people's *perceptions* of your actions create your reputation. Perception is reality, and successful networkers understand that reputations and careers can be built and ruined by the perceptions of others.

The rules of building a reputation may not always seem fair. First, reputation lags behind reality. Barring a major event that hits the news or the office grapevine, people's perceptions take time to adjust to any changes in your behavior. I once worked with a woman who arrived at work fifteen minutes late every day, and her tardiness had become an office joke. After Beverly made a big effort to change her ways and arrived promptly for about six weeks, she was annoyed to see that her officemates still rolled their eyes and checked the time when she arrived. It took her several months to shed her reputation for tardiness.

People may have long memories, but the Internet *never* forgets! It's an unavoidable part of today's world—potential employers and anyone else who wants to learn more about you will scour the Web, checking Google and social networking sites. In this world, a youthful indiscretion can resurface years later, and a reputation built over decades can be destroyed in a two-minute video on YouTube. And then there are the e-mail exchanges that go viral, creating unwanted fame or infamy for one or more participants. In one well-known case, a recent law school graduate accepted an offer at a local firm. A few days later, the firm changed its offer and the applicant ended up rejecting the position. An e-mail exchange best described as "snarky" ensued; that exchange was widely shared and even written about in the press as "how not to turn down a job."

Another way reputations aren't always "fair" is that some of your strengths and accomplishments may not be part of your public professional reputation. It's possible that people are unaware of all your skills. You cannot assume the people you know are aware of everything you are good at, so you must figure out a way to get your expertise out there. It's natural to pigeonhole people and define them by a job title or a few traits—you probably do this yourself when thinking of others. One way to expand the way others see you is to volunteer your services in your "unknown" skill.

RETHINKING YOUR REPUTATION

Because it is based on the perceptions of others, your reputation may seem out of your control. Still, there is much you can to do to manage and even enhance your reputation. Managing your reputation is not about "massaging" the facts to improve your image; it's not like sending out a glossy press release that makes you look better than you are. Remember, this book is about *authentic* networking, and that means being truthful. Managing your network is all about taking responsibility to manage yourself and your behavior.

Here's what you can do. First, find out what people are saying about you. Begin with the Internet. Googling yourself will reveal the public information that is out there. Make sure what comes up first on a search of your name is current, truthful, and positive! Take down any digital evidence of juvenile bad behavior. Keep online posts positive and constructive. If you have serious Internet image issues, professionals can advise you. The services of an "online reputation manager" (a new vocation for a new world!) will cost you several thousand dollars—so it's much better to avoid these problems in the first place if you can.

Continue your research in person. If you have a friend or acquaintance who is willing to be brutally honest, ask that person to share what others think of you.

? List the building blocks of your reputation on a piece of paper.
  ▷ What three things (personal or professional) are you most proud of?
  ▷ Why do people like to work with you?
  ▷ What would people say are the challenges of working with you?
  ▷ List three setbacks you have experienced. How did you recover?

Your reputation may include a damaging misperception that you must uncover and address. My client James was having a hard time getting past the second interview stage in spite of a strong résumé, appropriate experience, and excellent introductions and referrals. Finally, after he was turned down for yet another job that would have been a great fit for the organization and for him, I suggested that he go back to the hiring manager and ask for honest feedback and advice. The manager knew James only slightly, but he respected James' network and decided to be frank with him: He had heard through the grapevine that a number of former colleagues and direct reports thought James was too tough. Several people said he was a lone wolf who was out for himself and only "managed up." This came as a complete surprise to James because his last company had been in turmoil through a difficult restructuring; he had been focused on keeping it afloat. Armed with this knowledge, he was able to address the issue in future interviews, reframing his work history to cast it in a better and more accurate light. And do you remember Henry, whose reputation was tarnished through no fault of his own by association with a notorious acquiring firm? He corrected the misconception that he was a party to bad behavior when he changed the last entry on his résumé to read "Acquired by Tyco."

Sometimes a misconception does serious damage. When Ray Donovan, labor secretary under Ronald Reagan, was cleared of corruption charges, he famously inquired, "Which office do I go to, to get my reputation back?"

With luck, there are no misconceptions about you out there and the information circulating is correct. Still, your reputation may not be all that you desire it to be. Others may not see you the same way you see yourself. It is a psychological fact that we judge ourselves by our intentions, but others judge us by our actions. Your reputation is based on your achievements, not on what you hoped to accomplish; on what you said, not on what you meant to say. So, while you may see yourself as a pretty good person, the "word on the street" may be different. When you become aware of your personal blind spots and acknowledge your weak points, you are doing more than just being honest with yourself and others. Identifying your human faults or professional weaknesses is not just preparing a glib answer for an interview question.

Reputation is as much about how people feel about you as it is about the facts.

These traits are what people talk about. They are the "development opportunities" that your references will gently mention. These "areas for growth" can be detrimental to your reputation if you do not address them in your performance or personality. Look again at the building blocks you listed earlier and think of ways to improve your performance in weak areas.

Finally, as many public figures can attest, one big event can skew your reputation for better or worse, turning your carefully planned "snapshot" into an unfortunate candid photo. Warren Buffet summed it up: "It takes twenty years to build a reputation and five minutes to ruin it." And once it's ruined, recovery can take a long time. Career coach and author Adele Schelle reminds us that, "Everyone makes mistakes, and when you do you can wind up jeopardizing your job and even worse, your reputation. Whether you can salvage your reputation depends on the damage you have caused, your track record, and your willingness to do penance."

Take this advice to heart if your reputation needs repair. A string of failed projects, a damaging event, or even a history of bad behavior can be put in the past if you are willing to put in the effort to make things right. For example, James not only used the feedback he received to secure a new job; he took the time to seek out former colleagues and employees and rebuild those relationships. And when he landed a new position, he took advantage of his new-hire grace period to build credibility and improve his reputation in a new context.

Enhancing and protecting your reputation during a professional transition is especially challenging. Job transitions leave gaps on your résumé. People wonder why you "really" left that job, or what that chunk of time under "consultant" or "self-employed" really means. Be sure that you and members of your network can explain these gaps and provide credible and positive reasons why you are seeking new employment. Demonstrate by your attitude that you are moving on. And while you are in transition, be especially attentive to your networking behavior. Some people panic in transitions and revert to an "it's all about me" mindset. They make requests that are inappropriate in the context of the relationship, asking for too much, too fast. These behaviors burn bridges. Better to *build* bridges by attending to the relationships that can help you through these challenges.

Whatever your behavior, there is one thing you can be sure of: If you do not take the trouble to define yourself, others will. I once heard of a man whose last position had included downsizing a large, influential, and unprofitable company. He left few friends there and when he accepted a new job, his nickname, "Remorseless Robert," arrived in the office long before he did. That reputation made his transition a difficult one. In spite of being an intelligent and reasonable person, he never overcame his rocky beginnings or gained the trust of his new staff.

COMMUNICATING YOUR REPUTATION: ACCENTUATING THE POSITIVE

When a nickname or an office sound bite colors your reputation, you are letting others define you. It's far better to take control of your reputation and take responsibility for shaping the sound bite that sums you up for the world. What are the few words that can showcase your best qualities? Are you "the go-to guy"? A "cool head in a crisis"? A "networking guru"? It is useful to develop a short sentence—no more than about ten words—that will help you be perceived as you want to be. I call this creating a *signature statement*; it is different from the "elevator speech" that many career counselors encourage people to develop and that you will use in other contexts. The elevator speech is basically a sixty-second monologue in which you express what you can offer and what you are looking for. Your signature statement is shorter—more like a book's subtitle or a personal trademark that sets you apart from the crowd. It consists of one thing that someone should remember about you. Make it succinct and memorable so that it will be easy for others to share. There's no need to be embarrassed or to feel like you are bragging. On the contrary, if you can't talk about your strengths, how can you expect other people to? Besides, it's not bragging if it's true!

So, what might a signature statement sound like? Here are some examples I have heard over the years.

"I've covered all the bases in the industry."

"I know how to embrace leadership's vision and carry it forward."

"I manage complex situations."

"I can lead organizations through change."

? Take a moment now to draft your own signature statement. Don't worry about the exact phrasing now, but consider the one point you want to convey about yourself.

One way to start is to complete this sentence:

The people I work with see me as (a)_____

because I can _____

_____.

The second step in communicating your reputation is to talk to your network. Find out what people say when they talk about you. Is the message they convey the one you would like? Obviously, you don't want to put words in people's mouths. But you can help them help you by reminding them of aspects of your personality and experience that may not have been top-of-mind for them. If you are in a job search or in line for a promotion, it is especially important to talk with your references and remind them of relevant information and strengths. Building on the best that is within you, make your message positive and friendly and, above all, true. Remember it, repeat it, and practice it so that you don't leave your reputation to chance.

MINIMIZING THE NEGATIVE

Nobody is perfect. Everybody has some imperfections in his or her reputation. That's why knowing yourself and acknowledging your shortcomings is so important. You must accept the truth before you can address it or manage around it. Consider this common description: "He's a bright guy, but . . ." The phrase that follows that key word, *but*, is always negative and it carries more weight than the positive phrase that precedes it. ". . . but he can't see the forest for the trees." ". . . but he's only looking out for himself." ". . . but he really doesn't understand office politics."

How can you transform that negative part of your reputation? James, the executive who had managed his previous company through a major restructuring, faced this issue when former colleagues said, "He certainly knows how to make the numbers work, *but* all he really cares about is making the top brass happy." James was able to craft a message that mitigated this negative impression by preemptively sharing the difficult circumstances of his successful turnaround. He neutralized the negative by turning it in a positive direction.

Another way to manage your negative traits is to actively work around them. Again, this requires that you know yourself and acknowledge your weaknesses. You can manage around many "flaws" if you are willing to make the effort. For instance, if you tend to complete work late, set artificially early deadlines for yourself and stick to them. If

Your reputation is a work in progress.

you have a reputation for being unfriendly, make a point of stopping, looking people in the eye, and greeting them by name. If you have developed a reputation of not being a team player, be very public in sharing credit for your accomplishments.

You can also manage your weaknesses by delegating them or by sharing work with a colleague. Maybe your "but" statement is "She's great with the big picture, *but* loses it in the details." If you know this about yourself, work with an ally who enjoys sweating the details and getting them just right. Then you can neutralize that statement by saying, "I'm a 'big picture' type of person, *but* I know the importance of getting the details right. That's why I like working with people who are really good at execution."

YOUR REPUTATION AND YOUR NETWORK

Your reputation encapsulates what you stand for and the company you keep. Your network is an important part of your reputation. Remember in high school, when people might sum up a classmate with "He runs with the in crowd," or "She hangs out with the brainy kids"? Now, you might hear something like "George Jones speaks very highly of you," or "John told me that if I only had time to call one person, I should call you." In both cases, your network is part of what defines you.

Networking is at the crossroads of what you do best and the people you know best. The people in your network are an endorsement of you, your character, and your abilities. When you ask someone in your network for help, you get the benefit of her reputation. Use it wisely, because you are putting her reputation on the line as well as your own. When you achieve success, be sure to let some of the credit reflect back on the people who helped you. And remember to look for opportunities to help others. The wider your network, the more opportunities you will have to ask for and give help. When people talk about you, let them say, "He's always got his hand out to help."

The people in your network are an endorsement of you, your character, and your abilities.

Questions for Reflection

▷ What is the reputation of your industry? Your organization?

▷ What is your area of expertise?

▷ Is there anything you wish you could change about your reputation?

▷ Do people know your strengths and skills? Do you need to correct a misconception, or minimize a negative? If so, who in your network can help you?

▷ What is your signature statement? Can you say it in a confident and comfortable manner?

RELATIONSHIPS
The People You Meet along the Way

ON ANY GIVEN DAY, millions of people attend professional association meetings; millions more share a business luncheon; even more people make and receive cell phone calls; around the world, 1.7 billion people are active on the Internet. All of this goes to show that opportunities to meet and connect with people are endless and everywhere. But do they lead to real relationships? In the world of authentic networking, it's the *quality* of your network that counts. And quality networks are built on strong relationships that connect on a personal level as well as through business.

You can collect a long list of names by attending meetings, talking, or telephoning. You can fill a shoebox with business cards or a BlackBerry with contacts. But you'd still have nothing more than a long list of names. That list is meaningless unless it represents the give and take of real relationships, the outcome of getting to know one another as individuals, sharing similar interests, developing trust and respect, and offering and receiving help and input over time.

Relationships allow you to harness the intellectual capital of others. They bring you different perspectives and let you see the world from different points of view. Authentic networkers adopt an open and curious mindset that builds real-life long-lasting relationships. Their attitude is "Let me try to understand this person's values, needs, goals, and problems. Let me try to see the world his way and communicate that I am making that effort." Everyone has a network. What type? What size? How solid? Those are the important questions.

Think about someone for whom you would do anything—take his dog for the weekend (even though you're not a dog person), hold his hand through chemotherapy (even though you are afraid of hospitals), share the

Quality networks are built on strong relationships.

phone number of the busiest and best carpenter in town (even though he is working on your house), or recommend him to your best client, or even hire him in a minute for

the right opportunity. I'll be willing to bet this person takes up a lot more "space" in your life than does any contact listed in your insert-name-of-most-recent-contact-electronic-device. Relationships are your connections to the people in your work and life. And the more authentic you are, the stronger your relationships will be.

This lesson explores the importance of building lasting relationships in your network and will help you understand the different kinds of networking relationships. It explains why rethinking the value of relationships will help you to create new ones and strengthen or repair the ones you already have.

A relationship is an asset. Strong relationships are the blue-chip investment accounts of your network, or, as Harvard Business School professor and author Rosabeth Moss Kanter puts it in *World Class*, "Networks are options on future opportunities." You can invest in relationships and borrow from them, but only to the extent that you have built them up. Not long ago I shared a table at a breakfast meeting with a recently retired banker. We spent an hour talking about his experiences and his ideas about the future, exchanged cards, and parted with the usual offers of mutual assistance. Later that morning, by chance I ran into a professional friend I had known for most of his twenty years in the financial industry. That afternoon, I met with a new client who wanted to learn about current opportunities in banking; he asked me to suggest people he might contact.

Think about it. Which one of the two banking professionals I'd seen that day do you think I called on for this favor? I chose the one with whom I shared a history, someone I had spent time with on a nonprofit committee and seen in action, someone who knew his stuff and would be willing to listen to a person in the early stages of transition. (Later on, I became more acquainted with the first banker—and guess what, he knew my friend!) I believe both men would have been willing to help, but I chose my friend because every request, large or small, must be commensurate with the relationship between you and the person from whom you are asking the favor. Why? Because every time someone agrees to help you, that person puts *his* reputation and *his* relationships on the line, so a thoughtful request must reflect how well you know each other. Are you asking for the person's expertise, or his experience, or access to his network? Each presumes a very different level of knowledge about each other—very different account balances, if you will. Are you strangers? Acquaintances?

Authentic networkers build relationships without regard to age, power, income, or influence.

Colleagues? Close professional and personal friends? You must know and respect the boundaries of all your relationships—be clear, and even check their expectations, then adjust yours accordingly. Unlike jobs, college, careers, or home addresses, most relationships are permanent. And the stronger your relationships are, the stronger your network will be.

IT'S NOT WHAT YOU KNOW, IT'S WHO YOU KNOW

Texas governor Ann Richards knew how to get things done. She told an interviewer, "I don't know anyone who can do it on their own, nor do you have to, as long as you know where to get help." Your network extends your reach into the world, and the more diverse your network is, the greater your opportunity is to reach beyond your personal world. Authentic networkers see today's one-click-away world as an opportunity to appreciate and cultivate diverse relationships. Don't be overly concerned if reaching out to new people makes you uncomfortable. If you don't feel a little uncomfortable when you meet new people and extend your network, you probably aren't reaching far enough!

I have developed a tool I call "The Worlds I Travel In" to help people recognize how many networking worlds they touch. Here's how it works. List the twenty-six letters of the alphabet on the left-hand side of a sheet of paper. Now quickly jot down your professional "worlds" beside each letter. For example, next to *A*, you may write "accountants," "architects," "authors," and "actors"; next to *B*, "bankers" and "bakery owners"; next to *C*, "chemists." You get the idea. Your list will reflect your network. Remember to include your interests—yoga, historical preservation, sports—and hobbies—choral group, golf,

WORKSHEET: *The worlds I travel in*

A

B

C

D

E

F

G

H

I

J

K

L

etc...

even needlepoint. Especially needlepoint! When I first started my consulting practice, I was taking a weekly needlepoint class in Boston. Around that table sat eight high-level professional women, each seeking a different kind of success. The lawyer helped me with the legal affairs of my practice, the newspaper reporter wrote an article on the group that mentioned my practice, and the director of a large international organization invited me to lunch with her head of training in the executive dining room. Eight people who shared an interest and threads, connecting in a world most people would never see as having any career benefits. Yet those were two of the best possible hours each week for a newly launched independent consultant.

Once you have identified all the worlds you travel in, go back and list everyone you know in each of those categories—the more people and categories you can think of, the wider your world. If your network is spread across many professions, vocations, and interests, congratulations—keep up the good work! If not, I hope this exercise will help you realize that one of the best ways to meet people and build relationships is to connect your career interests with your life interests. When you do that you have the ability to add new relationships naturally all the time. Also remember to include people of all ages and cultures. Authentic networkers build relationships without regard to age, power, income, or influence. As Malcolm Forbes, long-time publisher of *Forbes* magazine, insisted, "There are no unimportant people." So, connect with all people at all levels—younger and less experienced employees, your colleagues and peers, and more senior staff. You can learn from all of them. And you never know where and how people will reappear in your life.

RELATIONSHIPS AREN'T ONE-SIZE-FITS-ALL

We have many kinds of relationships, and every one of them is unique. In her best-selling book *Necessary Losses*, Judith Viorst lists just a few examples of the relationships you will forge during your life. "Relationships—historical friends, crossroad friends, cross generational, friends when you call at 2:00 in the morning allow us to be ourselves and accept us that way. Convenience friends—the neighbors, officemates, largely routinely intersect with us. Exchange small favors, maintain public face and emotional distances." There is also a broad range of relationships from a networking perspective. Let's look at some in detail.

Core relationships are deep and important—the ones Judith Viorst says will take your call at 2:00 a.m. This is an elite group: the people who know your professional and personal goals, your hopes and concerns, your strengths, and what I like to call your "in-spite-ofs", as in "I like you in spite of the fact that you are always late to everything." If you are lucky and deal authentically with others, you will probably earn core relation-

> *Relationships are built and strengthened when people connect in person.*

ships with six to ten people over your lifetime. These powerful and usually reciprocal relationships comprise our deepest friendships. Alexandre Dumas, author of one of the world's greatest novels about friendship, *The Three Musketeers*, was speaking of these relationships when he defined friendship as "forgetting what one gives and remembering what one receives." You can expect to be in touch with members of your core group for a lifetime. They will take your call not only at 2:00 a.m. but 24/7, no matter where life takes you or them or how long it has been since you spoke. They will do anything for you, and if they can't personally do what you need, they will put themselves on the line with their networks for you. Turn to these *core* network friends when you need an advisory board because they know you best. They will support, encourage, and champion your efforts, just as you will do the same and more for them. Once these strong ties are created, it doesn't take much to sustain them, but you share bonds like this with only a small number of people.

Professional relationships, as you discovered when you completed the Worlds I Travel In worksheet, can include people from each functional area in your profession (don't worry about rank!) as well as from a wide range of other professions and industries. These relationships range from cordial nods in the hallways to close business friendships. Professional friendships depend on personal rapport; they are often built on exchanges of everything from work and business advice and useful information to goods and services. British sociologist Graham Allan has studied business friendship, and concludes, "Exchange is a basic human need. Relationships are not threatened when friends make use of one another provided it is clear that they are being used because they are friends and not friends because they are useful." Rotary International offers its members these rules of the road for actions that form and sustain successful business friendships (rules that could apply to all relationships). First, is it the truth? Second, is it fair to all concerned? Third, will it build goodwill and better friendships? And fourth, will it be beneficial to all concerned?

Professional relationships need to be actively maintained. Depending on the level of connectedness, you may keep in touch by attending professional meetings or making biannual "how-are-you-doing" phone calls, attending an annual lunch date, or sending regularly scheduled e-mails with information of interest (one of my clients has set up his computer to remind him when it's time to send these out to people in his business world network). Authentic networkers are always thinking about how they can provide introductions or business referrals to appropriate people in their networks; they seek out opportunities to ask for help on mutually beneficial professional and non-work-related issues. Who knows—that accountant in your network may be a fabulous former college baseball pitcher and be willing to join your summer league team. The key is not how often you make contact; the key is to keep in touch in a positive and friendly way. When a NASA mission lifted off on October 29, 1998, 77-year-old John Glenn (Navy pilot, astronaut, U. S. senator, author) was aboard as the subject of a study of space flight's effects on the elderly. When asked to describe his unrelenting efforts to persuade NASA to let him fly again, Glenn said simply, "Let's just say, I kept adequately in touch."

Social relationships—neighbors, people from church and civic groups, club members, families of your children's friends, and so on—also vary widely in their type and depth. But each social relationship plays a role in our life and the lives of our chosen communities. Too often we take these relationships for granted and expect they will be there when we need them. Giving plays a big role here, but it doesn't have to take much effort or time. All that's needed is a sense of caring—picking up the newspaper from your neighbor's driveway when the family is away, buying a raffle ticket from a school club or church group, or taking dinner to a person who is ill or in crisis. These simple acts of reaching out, often unnoticed, can build social relationships and stronger communities.

Casual relationships are fashioned from small exchanges with strangers. They develop—over the course of a few hours of waiting in an airport or a few months of buying coffee at the same shop—into friendly acquaintances. Don't underestimate the value or power of casual relationships or of serendipity. A client shared this illustration of the "you never know" factor as he described the best introduction he ever received during a job search. Because he knew his search would take time, Paul decided to volunteer at a local shelter, helping men who lacked access to company-sponsored job search advice and assistance. During a session in which he was explaining how difficult it can be to make a good connection, he revealed that he had been trying every senior-level person he knew to get an introduction to a certain very prominent and respected business executive. At the end of the session, one of the participants, an unemployed carpenter, came up and said, "I can introduce you." Paul said, "I thanked the guy nicely and thought 'no way!' Then he went on to tell me that he has a band; ten years ago they were playing at a wedding and this guy came up and asked to play the drums during one of the sets. Well, ever since, this fellow shows up on a regular basis at the band's weekly practices. Yup, you guessed it. He was referring to Mr. Prominent, Impossible-to-Get-an-Introduction-to Executive. I learned a big lesson that day. I thought I was the one 'giving' help, but in reality . . ."

My father-in-law, a born everyday networker, sums it up: "Casual encounters are as important as deep friendships. They make life pleasant, be it the clerk in the store where I buy my morning paper, the woman I buy my coffee from, or the bus driver I meet every day on my way to work."

What might develop through our networking efforts if we all took responsibility for making every encounter a positive one? Anything! If you are open to new people and experiences, even random encounters can bring pleasant surprises. My co-author shared an example from her own experience on a recent long flight. After some polite small talk Perry and her seatmate Chris discovered several mutual interests. Perry was especially happy to be able to share contact information within a specialized profession that Chris was prospecting—something Chris never expected to learn on Southwest Flight 592!

Finally, as we consider casual relationships, remember that there are people you know, and who know you, only *by reputation*. You may be in the same industry and professional groups, or you may have friends in common.

If you have ever met someone for the first time and heard "So-and-so has told me so much about you—I feel like I already know you!" you know how it's possible to have a relationship with someone you have never or barely met. If you want to take a relationship of this kind to the next level, ask yourself a few questions. How much do you really know about this person? What has he heard or discovered about you? In what context does she know you? The answers to these questions should guide you as you build your relationships. As stated in an earlier lesson, reputations are often based on perceptions. Authentic networkers seek to validate, through actions and behavior, the positive things that have been said and that others believe about us.

Besides being different in scope, intensity, and longevity, relationships fill different roles in your life. Some people will act as *guides* through unknown territory. Some are *allies*, no matter what. Others are *catalysts* who nudge you to action or *door openers* who can widen your circle of acquaintances. If you are in a job search, you probably hope to be introduced to a *decision maker*, but don't dismiss the *data provider*, a person who can share the critical background or insider information you need. And remember, you too can play the role of guide, ally, catalyst, door opener, decision maker, or data provider in your relationships with others. Which roles are you playing now? Go back to your Worlds I Travel In worksheet (page 48). How are your roles different for the different relationships in your network?

CREATING RELATIONSHIPS

Authentic networkers know that meeting people and building new relationships may not come naturally, but it isn't rocket science. What I have learned from twenty-plus years of workshops, speeches, and clients is that relationships are built when hellos turn into conversations. Stop here and think about the number and variety of people you have met and may meet in the future.

? How many people will you meet today? This week? How many will you
meet in a month, a year, a lifetime?
  ▷ Think of the people you went to school with—grammar school, high
    school, college, or workshops and seminars; people from your previous
    and current workplaces.

▷ Think about people who share your religious affiliation, nationality, ethnic background or culture; people who belong to your social clubs, organizations, agencies, or societies.

▷ Think about people you do volunteer work or play sports with; people with season tickets to the events you attend; people who share your hobbies.

▷ Think about people who live in your current or former neighborhood; people you've met on vacation; people who share your hobbies; people you know through friends or family.

▷ Think about people who provide services for you—doctors, dentists, lawyers, repair people, service people, bankers, store clerks, mail carriers.

Obviously, the list goes on and on! To meet even more people, take a walk with your dog or a child or with a colleague at lunchtime. You will be amazed at the number of positive encounters you will have, each potentially expanding your network by adding new and varied connections. Children and dogs are guaranteed to elicit smiles and pleasant conversations that can develop into cordial acquaintances. And that lunchtime stroll will give you the chance to get to know your colleague better and perhaps run into others along the way.

When you meet a person you'd like to know better, look for common experiences or acquaintances. It is easiest to start a relationship when you have something in common; the most basic building blocks of relationships are the things you share with others. Dog walkers, for example, are known for networking as they walk and scoop—everyone at the dog park shares a love of dogs, and dog antics make an easy conversation starter. The *New York Times* took note of this in "Petworking," a feature that describes the city dog runs as "'an open-air caffeine cocktail party where all the guests are dressed for latrine duty . . . the dogs go off leash and people stand around with their coffee talking away, and eventually you find out what everyone does." What a natural way to get beyond knowing the dog's name to greeting the owner by name—and then to begin talking about other common interests. You'll soon discover an obvious truth: People who walk their dogs happen to know other people who know other people who know of openings and opportunities. "In other words," reports the *Times*, "while upwardly mobile New

Yorkers are surfing Internet job boards and paying top dollar for résumé services, some excellent leads may be at the end of the leash."

While the opportunity to build a relationship begins as soon as you meet someone you would like to know better, it takes time to build any lasting relationship, be it in a dog park, on a golf course, at a professional association meeting, or in the workplace. In fact, research suggests that it takes five encounters to move a relationship to the next level. For example, in your networking efforts, you might bump into a person casually, or call or send a letter introducing yourself. The second encounter might be a follow-up note or call, which can be followed by a more formal friendly meeting. After sending a thank-you note (the fourth encounter), you will probably find that you connect at a deeper and more personal level when you meet for the fifth time. The definition of "relationship" implies a minimum—more than one meeting or call—but no maximum. Building relationships is a process, not an isolated activity.

When you are considering career development and advancement, it's especially important to take advantage of opportunities to build some kinds of relationships before you need them. Networking is always cited as the number one way to find a job, and yes, a great network will yield great results. But how many of us have the name of a search firm or an executive recruiter listed on our Worlds I Travel In worksheet? Professional recruiters are in the business of finding the right person for the right job—truly a relationship business. A recruiter can be an important professional relationship to build and nurture over the course of your work life. Yet many people never give recruiters a thought until they are out of work; then they call them and expect to be treated like a long lost friend or a dream-come-true job candidate. Consider how much more pleasant and mutually beneficial it is to maintain a cordial acquaintance with a few key recruiters, building enough rapport to comfortably call or be called to chat about industry trends, to learn what's going on in the marketplace, or to refer appropriate candidates.

Human resources professionals are also important people with whom to maintain relationships. They are up-to-date on the latest in talent management and workplace trends, and have a sense of recruiting needs inside and outside their organizations. They can advise and guide you through your company's career leadership and professional development programs and policies. They know about executive education or graduate school tuition assistance programs. And when work and life seem out of balance, they may be able to assist by finding the appropriate resources. Many people ignore these two key relationships or take them for granted. Don't make that mistake.

WHAT WORKS: ONLINE OR IN PERSON

The Internet is a wonderful thing, but please observe this caveat: Keep it "real." Technical tools are great for conveniently arranging life: making plans, letting others know you will be late, and updating friends. Many people rely more and more on text messages, abandoning the telephone for simple exchanges and avoiding voice mail entirely. And a savvy user can exploit blogging, Twitter, and other tools to create a personal brand for himself that extends far beyond his physical presence. But regardless of how easy it may be to connect and keep in touch through the Internet, don't rely solely on social networking sites such as MySpace, Facebook, LinkedIn, or Friendster for building relationships. True, these sites do connect people, and many of these connections have led to opportunities or developed into relationships. But too often these tools simply become tracking and contact systems; they don't create or foster long-lasting, real relationships all by themselves. Many business articles extol the benefits of social media, yet still acknowledge that relationships are built and strengthened when *people* connect *in person* versus online. Even technology gurus do their networking face to face. *BusinessWeek* reported that "During the holidays last year, [entrepreneurs] Aydin Senkut and Elad Gil gathered 50 of their friends at a health-food restaurant in Palo Alto . . ." while Dan Schawbel, Millennial Branding founder and a member of *Inc. Magazine*'s "30 Under 30" top young entrepreneurs, concluded an article on different online tools with "But now I'm realizing how important face-to face contact is—it's more powerful than any online networking."

RELATIONSHIPS FOR THE LONG HAUL

Once a person is in your network, he or she can be in your network forever. Over time, you will get new jobs and leave old ones, but the relationships you forge will stay with you. You may see each other less frequently or in different circumstances, but as long as you both have positive feelings for each other the connection will be ongoing, even if it's not active. Remember our everyday networking principle: Networking doesn't just happen; it takes personal effort. *The Power of Everyday Networking* was written to help you find a new way to network, one in which building relationships is a priority. When you network authentically, you take responsibility for reaching out and standing by people in good times and bad. You base more relationships on the everyday acts of caring—a card, a short phone call, an interesting news article—rather than on filling an impressive social calendar or landing a corner office. You build on the things you have in common and learn from the differences you discover.

Good relationships are ongoing, and the frequency and quality of connection doesn't change when you need help. People know when they are being used for short-term personal gain, or when you only contact them when you need something. So, let them know they are important to you by checking in regularly with a call, an e-mail, or a lunch date at a frequency that feels comfortable to both parties. Follow Norman Vincent Peale's familiar advice: "Never miss an opportunity to offer support or to say congratulations. When they help you, follow up quickly with a 'thank you' and let them know the outcome of their efforts."

Let people know they are important to you.

Good relationships endure even when the circumstances that fostered them change, because relationships don't end, they evolve. Switching jobs or moving cross-country are not reasons to lose touch. If you have let a relationship lapse, you can renew it with a phone call or through LinkedIn (the other day I was delighted to hear from someone I consulted with almost twenty years ago). Just call and catch up. There's no need to apologize for your recent absence. The reason for your call is to demonstrate your interest in the other person. Ask what he or she has been up to *before* sharing your own news. After all, the people you forge relationships with are people you want to know more about.

Great networks are built on great relationships. Relationships make our days more pleasant and productive. We all rely on other people to help us through the day. Let's end with a word from twentieth-century African American tennis champion Althea Gibson, who summed it up when she said, "No matter what accomplishments you make, somebody helped you." That somebody is more than likely one of the many relationships you have built in your network!

Questions for Reflection

▷ How many categories did you easily fill in on your Worlds I Travel In worksheet (page 48)? What others would you like to add?

▷ Who is in your core network? When was the last time you let them know how important they are to your professional and personal success?

▷ Think about a casual acquaintance who has developed into a close member of your network. How and why did this happen?

▷ How do you use social networking tools? List some everyday ways they enhance your connections and strengthen your networking relationships.

RAPPORT

Make a Connection with Every Interaction

AT A RECENT ASSOCIATION meeting, I found myself seated next to a person I knew slightly. After exchanging names and realizing we had met before, I asked about him and his job to get the conversation rolling. Then I asked about the company he ran, its location, and its services. Finding that line of conversation going nowhere, I turned to outside interests and discovered he was an amateur chef. So I asked how he got into cooking, what cuisine he enjoyed most, and what his must-have kitchen tools were. Through four courses and coffee, I asked questions and he answered them— some briefly and others in a poker-faced monologue. His replies never went beyond answering my questions, and he never asked a question about me— in fact, he never asked any questions at all! Needless to say, I did not feel that we had established rapport by the end of the meal. I wondered if it was me; but then I recalled that by accepting and attending this event, *he* had a responsibility to make an effort to converse. I decided to say, "Nice to hear all is going well with you," and skipped dessert!

The ability to communicate is not only vital to your professional success; it affects your personal life and your reputation too. My dinner partner lacked a communication skill that, while useful, is rarely found today: the skill of establishing rapport, whether for the brief time you spend in another's company or for long-term relationships that expand your network.

Organizations run on the spoken word: conversations, interviews, meetings, phone calls, debates, requests, debriefings, announcements, business development, and speeches. In addition to words, gestures, facial expression, tone of voice, silence, posture, and body language profoundly affect people even when they are not aware of them. How you speak and how you listen play an important part in determining where and how far you go. We all judge people to some extent by how well they communicate, in part because we know that every verbal and nonverbal message they send to colleagues, customers, clients, in job interviews, and in networking is an expression of their attitudes. Communicating with warmth, interest, and integrity is the foundation of rapport.

Notice that I said that establishing rapport is a *skill*. It's not an innate talent or something that depends on "chemistry" between people. It is a communication skill used by authentic networkers and, like all skills, it can be learned and improved (remember our principles of networking). Rapport is based on the ability to make meaningful social conversation, not just small talk. You build rapport when your attitude is "I wonder what this person is interested in," instead of "Let me tell you all about me." Authentic networkers who aren't born with this kind of enthusiasm, or who are anxious when talking to strangers, develop strategies to get over their awkwardness and build rapport. One is to demonstrate sincere interest in others—by maintaining eye contact, smiling, and asking questions. This is how my dinner partner dropped the ball: He showed up, he sat at the table, but he neglected his *responsibility* to initiate or try to make any meaningful conversation with me or the other attendees at our table.

Understand the power of asking questions.

Rapport is a great way to build and strengthen one-on-one relationships. In this lesson you will learn why. You will also learn how a few simple communication skills can make building rapport with others a more comfortable process, even if it doesn't come naturally. Finally, this lesson explains how authentic networkers use rapport to connect with their networks, to keep in touch, and when necessary, to ask for help. Remember our third principle of networking: A network is created to serve its members.

? Before you continue reading, ask yourself the following questions. Jot down the answers in your notebook.

▷ How comfortable are you when you talk to others?

▷ Do you take a genuine interest in people you meet, or do you feel that talking with them is an interruption?

▷ What two or three initial questions do you ask when you want to learn more about someone?

▷ How do you pick up clues about what is important to others, and then respond?

Every person is more than his or her business persona. We all have a hobby or an interesting background; do you discover it and show your interest by asking to learn more through a follow-up question? Or, like my dinner partner, do you miss out on opportunities to build rapport? Authentic networkers enjoy spending time with people. They know they don't have to become best friends with a person to enjoy talking with him or her. Even when they strongly disagree, authentic networkers find a way to keep an open mind, have a pleasant exchange, and learn from the conversation. This attitude respects and enhances any relationship. It is what turns casual contacts into real connections, fosters a wide range of diverse relationships, and allows your network to grow.

And, as we learned in the previous lesson, authentic networking is all about relationships, about who we know and how well we know them. It's about leaving short-term and transactional thinking and actions behind and replacing them with long-term relationship building. Consider this exchange from *The Wall Street Journal*.

QUESTION: Most advice on networking doesn't say what I should talk about with people I contact. Do people just call each other to say "Hi, how are things going these days?" Please provide some input.

ANSWER: Unless you're calling a good friend or a relative, you probably won't get far with the kind of an opening statement such as, "Hi, how are things going." Networking is really just relationship building. It's more about connections with other people than about what you say to them initially. Once you have established a relationship, the rest takes care of itself.

What is the first step to building a real-world relationship? Rapport.

DEVELOPING RAPPORT

For many people, building rapport begins as a social skill. Some people have the natural ability to talk with everyone they meet and feel comfortable in the process. If this doesn't come naturally to you, it might help to prepare yourself with some "conversation starters." Come up with two or three things you can safely say to anyone: What books are on your nightstand? What kinds of music do you listen to? Center your talk on the other person—after all, conversation is a dialogue, not a monologue! Author Bob Burg puts it this way: "You meet someone somewhere and the average person will start talking about himself. But the fact is, at that moment they are not interested in you and your business. Instead, turn the conversation around so that 99.9% of the conversation is focused on the other person."

Make the conversation about the other person first, and you second. Always be positive; never be negative in your comments, gossip about an organization, or talk unfavorably about people who are not in the room. A tendency to gossip is a common trap, and it is easy to fall into it when you are uncomfortable, but it will always reflect unfavorably on you. And if you discover you have mutual friends, acknowledge the type of connection you each have and say something positive about the person. Then steer the conversation back to getting to know more about each other.

Next, let the conversation expand beyond work; don't let a person's title and industry define the conversation. People are more than their credentials and résumés. The real exchange lies at the level of conversation beyond reputation and what do you do for work; that's where you can find a world of lasting connections. You can talk about local, national, and international events, culture, sports—even politics and finance as long as you keep the conversation courteous and respectful of everyone's views. Who knows, you might even learn something that will change your own way of thinking.

Finally, the best way to develop rapport is to understand the power of asking questions. John W. Gardner, a statesman and author of two books on leadership, advised, "Don't set out in life to be an interesting person. Set out to be an interested person." Asking broad, open-ended, and thoughtful questions ("Why did you choose to hike the Appalachian Trail during your transition?") demonstrates your interest in the other person and signals that you are paying attention to what she is saying. A good question sets the tone and naturally encourages a back-and-forth debate or exchange of ideas while leaving the speaker free to say as much or as little as he or she wants. Questions needn't be complex; in fact, authentic networkers keep questions simple and ask only one question at a time. After all, if you ask a two-part question, people tend to either answer only the second part or not answer the part you want to pursue.

Listen carefully for responses that provide opportunities for intelligent follow-up questions. Asking follow-up questions can make the difference between being seen as someone who is really listening and being seen as a game show host who peppers people with random questions. A follow-up question shows that you are making a genuine effort to know more about the person—as an individual. It helps you take the topic from the category of "nice to know" information to a personal level of "nice to know *you*." Follow-up questions also help you to be in charge of the pace; they keep the conversation on track and bring it to a timely, mutually beneficial conclusion.

Do you have a particular objective for your conversation? If you want to get specific information, tailor your initial questions to meet your aims; it will help you to assess the other person's knowledge and interest in discussing it. Different types of questions invite different answers. An open-ended question (one that cannot be answered with "yes" or "no") will open up the discussion without closely defining the topic. For example,

Concentrate on the speaker's message, both verbal and nonverbal.

"What do you enjoy most about your job?" or "What brought you to this event tonight?" A closed question will elicit a "yes" or "no" and possibly some supporting details. "Do you think the Red Sox will go all the way this year?" A fact-finding question will draw out information on a particular subject ("What does the new law mean for your industry?"), and the follow-up question will elicit more information or an opinion ("So, what new challenges does it present?").

People will share more if your questions are nonthreatening and framed without negative phrases such as "Why didn't you...?", "How could you...?", "Aren't you...?", or "I can't believe you didn't..." No matter what kind of question you ask or statement you make, give the person a chance to respond to it! Try silently counting to ten (or even twenty) before speaking. This will give the other person an opportunity to get his or her ideas out and give you the chance to listen for where to guide the conversation and what question to ask next.

LISTENING

The first step to good listening is to stop talking! OK, nowadays the first step is to turn off your cell phone whenever you are in the company of others. Listening is a powerful communication skill and one of the most effective ways to establish rapport, yet studies show that only about 10 percent of us actually listen intelligently and purposefully. Listening is hard work; it requires that we stop talking, concentrate, and pay attention. That isn't always easy in today's fast-moving and stressful world, where your mind is often going in several different directions at once. It's difficult to give your full attention and time to another person when your mind wants to review your to-do list, plan the presentation you're giving tomorrow, or make that phone call you meant to make yesterday.

Many people also fall into the habit of tuning out others as soon as they think they have grasped the gist of the message. They stop listening and begin mentally preparing their own statements or rebuttals. The result is that people end up talking *at* one another rather than *with* one another, making plenty of relevant points, but not really communicating or connecting.

Another listening challenge is the difference between our speaking and thinking speeds. Most people speak at about 200 words per minute, but they *think* at about four times that speed. What do their brains do with all that extra time? Usually they mull around looking for facts and a point or two of agreement or argument, and then prepare a response, rebuttal, or counterpoint. It takes a real effort to resist using that extra "brain space" in this way.

Stephen Covey observes in *The Seven Habits of Highly Effective People* that "Most of us love to yak about ourselves. While others are speaking, many people don't pay complete attention. Instead, they just bide their time until they can jump in with their own anecdote."

They are *hearing*, which is not the same as *listening*. Listening involves paying attention to what is said between the lines; a true listener understands not only the words, but also the attitudes, needs, and motivations behind the speaker's words. And this is what we need to build rapport in the relationship.

Ironically, modern communication gadgets often make listening even harder. Observe people's behavior the next time you attend a meeting. Many rush in with a cell phone to their ears, so absorbed in those conversations that they neglect to greet their colleagues or introduce themselves to others. Once they sit down, they attempt "small talk" as they read a last-minute e-mail or send one last *important* text. What about you? Do you really think people don't see your eyes darting up and down, or your hands punching keys while they are speaking? And this behavior isn't confined to the workplace. You'll see it at social events and family dinners. How about a college classroom, where students who pay thousands in tuition spend their time surfing, e-mailing, and texting while pretending to take notes? A friend in her twenties recalls having dinner with six former classmates. As they sat down, each placed her cell phone next to her plate. Since when did a cell phone become part of a table setting? My friend looked around the table and said, "We are here to talk to one another; shut off your cell phones and put them away." You go, girl!

Networks show their real value when they serve their members.

To be a good listener, turn off all the internal and external distractions and focus your mind on being present. Give the conversation your full attention and involvement. If your mind goes off on a tangent, quickly reel it in by repeating a comment or asking a pertinent question. You can do this when you concentrate on the speaker's message, both verbal and nonverbal. Give the other person time to talk without interrupting, evaluating, defending yourself, or analyzing what is being said. Stay neutral. Take what you hear at face value without making assumptions, judging, or "politely" correcting the speaker. Don't give in to distractions or look at the clock.

You'll build rapport when the speaker is convinced that you're listening. Your nonverbal cues make your listening skills—or lack of them—obvious. The signals you send indicate whether you're really listening—a positive tone to your voice, open gestures and facial expressions, looking the speaker in the eye, leaning forward when it's appropriate—or just faking it. You also provide positive acknowledgment by nodding and responding to key points with information that adds value. You can also signal that you're listening by periodically checking for understanding. Restate the message in your own words and ask if you heard it correctly. "So, you're recommending more market research, is that right?" If the speaker says "no," ask for clarification—again showing you want to listen, and learn.

? How able a listener are you? Complete the following sentences to assess your listening skills.
  ▷ I find it easiest to listen to people who are . . .
  ▷ When I really want to listen I . . .
  ▷ When I'm not interested in listening I . . .
  ▷ In order to listen carefully I . . .
  ▷ I show that I am listening by . . .

IF YOU DON'T ASK, HOW CAN THEY SAY YES?

Remember, networks show their real value when they serve their members. Your network is your best career management resource; it is made to be tapped, but it is only available to you if it is active. The skill of rapport makes it easier to *keep in touch* with the many different relationships you develop over the course of your career. The open, honest, and on-going communication that rapport fosters lets you reach out to others without worrying about when or how often you call; it frees you to catch up on what's been going on in one another's worlds, to reconnect and deepen your relationships. If you have built a network based on rapport, you can do what the popular cell phone carrier tells you: "Just pick up the phone and call someone—in your network."

Once you've developed rapport, you can ask for what you need—advice, information, or referrals. Just be sure your relationship has the level of trust that supports your request. You should only ask for things you can reasonably expect to be given. What you can ask for depends on the strength of the relationship and on the ability and willingness of the other person to respond to your request. So, be sure your relationship is solidly in place before asking for help or making a request.

As in so many aspects of networking, taking responsibility plays a big part in knowing what to ask for and how to make a request from someone in your network. After all, every time you ask for something you open yourself up to a possible "No, not now," or to feelings of personal rejection. To avoid these, remember the tips offered in the lesson on responsibility, such as using positive language and a confident tone of voice. Be clear on the purpose of your call and follow the three rules of making requests: Know exactly what you want, be willing to ask for what you want, and ask the right person for the right thing—ask for something that person *can* and *will* do. Is it possible for the person to fulfill the request? Convenient?

If you make it easy for the person to grant your request, your request will strengthen and maintain your relationship. Research shows that a person who grants a favor feels more positive toward the person receiving the favor than before the request was made. Benjamin Franklin provides an example of the "favor effect" in his autobiography. Franklin decided he would win the friendship of a fellow legislator in the Pennsylvania House, a political opponent who had been personally hostile to him. Even though Franklin and his fellow legislator were political enemies, they shared a love of knowledge and books. This laid the groundwork for trust.

Franklin succeeded in winning his opponent over by asking for a special favor. "Having heard that he had in his library a certain very scarce and curious book, I wrote a note to him expressing my desire of perusing that book and requesting he would do me the favor of lending it to me for a few days." The man immediately sent Franklin the book, which Franklin returned in a few days with a note of thanks. The relationship then changed dramatically. "When we next met in the House he spoke to me (which he had never done before), and with great civility; and he ever after manifested a readiness to serve me on all occasions, so that we became great friends."

The favor effect works because people *want* to help and give you what you need to be successful; they want to be thought of as someone who has made a difference both in general and to you personally. But they also want to be asked. The legendary Boston politician and former speaker of the house, Tip O'Neill, lost his first city council election by just over 200 votes; one of those voters was someone O'Neill had known his entire life. Why didn't she vote for him? He never asked her to. From that experience, O'Neill created the "Mrs. O'Brien Rule": People, even your neighbor from across the street, want to be asked for their votes.

Some people fail to ask because they fear putting people on the spot—a concern that can be confused with legitimate courtesy. Rest assured: People will let you know how they feel by their words and actions. They may respond with a positive and active promise of help: "Certainly, let me make that call. I'll get right back to you by e-mail with the information." Or they may tell you straight away, "No, I can't do it." Or they may nod vaguely, but not follow through, letting you know this is something they are unable or unwilling to do. Whatever the response, it is there for a reason; don't judge, but do step back and assess what you asked for, how you asked for it, and why you asked them. They have let you know how they feel, and that's what authentic networkers want to know. It's much better to know how they feel than to walk away with unfulfilled expectations or holding a grudge.

People want to be asked.

Even when you are making a request, it is easy to make it a two-way street by finding the opportunities to give back. You can always end your request with "What's going on in your world? What do you need? What are your goals, challenges, and opportunities? How can I help you?"

FAIRness

A successful networking request is about asking for feedback, advice, information, referrals, or leads, with the reasonable expectation of receiving an answer of "yes." The authentic networker asks only for the things others can and will give. I call it behaving FAIRLY.

FEEDBACK: The chance to hear in someone's own words what he or she feels you can do is a gift. Feedback helps you reflect and improves your understanding. Sometimes people mistake feedback for criticism. Leave yourself open to the possibility that any criticism is constructive and made in good faith. Don't justify yourself and don't interrupt. You asked for feedback because you believed there was something valuable to be learned, so listen carefully. Remember James, the executive whose prospects were clouded by misconceptions about his past behavior? He listened, and it helped him land a job.

ADVICE: Advice is intelligence gathering. Ask for advice when you are looking for ideas and trying to think outside the box. If you gain a wide range of advice, you'll benefit from a number of different opinions.

INFORMATION: Your network can provide all sorts of information. Use your network to gather data and facts about people you'll be meeting or would like to meet.

REFERRAL: It's a myth that people don't like to give referrals. They feel good about giving referrals because they're helping someone out. It is true, though, that you typically don't get referrals from "contacts." Referrals are more typically obtained from long-term relationships, people you've worked with over time and with whom you've developed trust. These people will introduce you to someone they know, pass your name along to their network, or tell you, "The guy you need to see is . . ."

LEADS: While referrals are personal introductions to individuals, leads direct you to concrete job opportunities. You are more likely to get leads from someone who knows your value to an organization and with whom you have developed a relationship based on genuine rapport than from a person you have just met.

YES: *Y* stands for the most important word: *Yes*. All requests should be shaped in a way that ensures a "Yes, I can and will help you" response. So, before you ask, be clear about your expectations so that you can be confident there is a way the other person can and will help. To avoid putting the other person in the position of saying "no," don't ask for too much. Don't ask for something that puts a burden on the person or on someone he or she knows.

And when you get that "yes," be it for feedback, advice, or a referral, take it. Instead of saying, "Oh, that won't work, I've tried it," follow up on it and report back. Honor the relationship by promptly thanking the person who referred you and return the favor with an introduction of your own if possible. Regardless of the outcome, share the results with the person who gave the referral. And be especially scrupulous when dealing with your new contact, because failure to live up to commitments that grow out of referrals will damage *two* reputations.

CONNECTING WITH STRANGERS

Developing and maintaining rapport with people you already know is important—but the way to broaden and deepen your network is to meet new people and convert strangers into connections. There are many ways to meet new people. Joining professional, civic, and volunteer organizations is an excellent way, because they are based on your own authentic interests.

Make interactions with strangers as comfortable as possible. Put them at ease while appearing comfortable yourself. Authentic networkers introduce themselves, and then take personal responsibility for guiding the conversation and asking questions that will lead to finding common ground: a shared hobby or travel interest; a common profession or educational background.

You may think, "I'm shy. I can't do that." Well, shy doesn't mean dull. You have plenty to offer. Just follow my A, B, C formula: Accept your nerves, Believe positively, and Converse naturally. Remember, it's not unusual to be tongue-tied, but once you get past this fear you'll have the foundation for a conversation and for potentially building a relationship. You may not think you have anything in common with a stranger, but how can you know until you reach out?

As the *Wall Street Journal* questioner mentioned earlier in the chapter learned in the response to the question: "Relationships are developed most easily when you have something in common with the other person. Find commonalities that you can build on before you meet or pick up the telephone." How can you do that? Check your network—you may know people in common. Ask a mutual friend to make an introduction. This will do more than open the door; it will give you something to talk about when you do meet. The response sums it up, "You may not get job leads, referrals, or any other help you want at the beginning. The rewards usually come later. Just be genuine and focus on how you can help the other party."

In this *Wall Street Journal* Q&A exchange, it sounds like the relationship started with a cold call, the most feared of all networking experiences, even for authentic networkers. Cold-calling involves going outside your own network to make requests of any kind. Most people truly hate making and receiving cold calls, so it is important to be as prepared as possible and to make the call worthwhile for both parties.

To "warm up" a cold call, script your introduction with a brief explanation of what you do and why you are calling. Scripting the call may seem artificial, but it is really an organized way of building rapport and getting to the point (important in any cold call). Jotting down your bullet points will clarify the call for you, and having some open questions based on your research will help to engage the person you have called. The better you understand yourself and your needs, the more effective you will be. Scripting will also help you pace yourself and give you a point of reference if you get off track. But be careful not to over-script: You must be real, believe what you say, and listen for cues from the person you have called.

The way to broaden and deepen your network is to meet new people.

The stress of making a cold call or engaging a stranger in conversation has a surprising side benefit. Everyone knows cold calls, job interviews, and other high-stakes conversations with strangers are stressful. When people see us handle ourselves well under stress, they become aware of an added dimension to our professionalism. We aren't just another job seeker, or someone looking to quickly grow our Rolodex, but someone with the depth of character that comes from taking responsibility for our own success.

NETWORKING ON THE NET

Nowadays, everybody is "networking" on Facebook, LinkedIn, and other Internet social networking sites. It seems so easy to add friends and contacts—click a few buttons and *voilà*! One hundred new friends! But don't confuse making digital contacts with building rapport. Connecting at a conversational level is vital even as technology plays an increasingly important role in our lives, workplaces, and homes. (Remember the restaurant get-together mentioned earlier, where fifty of Aydin Senkut and Elad Gils' high-tech friends gathered *in person*.) As Edward Hallowell, author, psychiatrist, and instructor at Harvard Medical School, explains it, "We need to experience what I call the human moment, an authentic psychological encounter that can happen only when two people share the same physical space . . . The human moment has two prerequisites: People's physical presence and their emotional and intellectual attention . . . Human moments require energy." Human moments, even brief conversations, help you to build rapport and strengthen relationships.

As Hallowell puts it, "You can pay attention to someone over the telephone, for instance. But somehow phone conversations lack the power of true human moments." This is true of all technology-assisted conversations, largely because nonverbal cues such as the way you dress, your manners, posture, and eye contact are in short supply. In person, you have many points of reference to size someone up: She knows her stuff; is respectful and courteous; plays by the rules; takes care of her appearance, and so on. Online, you don't have nearly as much information and it's easier to spin it. To develop rapport and a relationship, you need more data points, and the people evaluating you do, too. A well-known *New Yorker* cartoon hits the nail on the head: "On the Internet, nobody knows you're a dog." Authentic networkers learn and leverage different media for the things each one is best suited for. There is nothing better than being able to e-mail 24/7 or send a quick text (versus playing telephone tag) to set up a time for a phone call or to let someone know traffic has held you up. What's important is that when you use technology, you use it because it adds something to the relationship and serves the other person, not just because it's more convenient for *you*. The table on the next page outlines the information that is available in conversations pursued through different media.

If you do use social networking sites or message boards, be selective. Nobody believes you really have thousands of legitimate links. And be careful! We've all heard the stories of people who met the love of their life, found a perfect business partner, or launched a lucrative business from home. But we've heard horror stories too, and not just about Russian bank scams. Recently, the blogosphere was abuzz with the story of a young man's post about a new job on a public message board: "I don't like the company and I'll be bored, but the money's great and the commute's short." The hiring manager

Available Cues	In Person	Video Conference or Skype	Phone Call	Voice Mail	Letter	Online/E-mail
Appearance	Yes	Yes	No	No	L*	No
Handshake, touch	Yes	No	No	No	No	No
Body language	Yes	Yes	No	No	No	No
Facial expression	Yes	Yes	No	No	No	No
Smile	Yes	Yes	Yes	Yes	No	No
Tone of voice	Yes	Yes	Yes	Yes	No	No
Literal meaning of words	Yes	Yes	Yes	Yes	Yes	Yes
Implied meanings and humor	Yes	Yes	Yes	L	L	L
Give and take	Yes	Yes	Yes	No	No	L

L = Limited

frequented the same discussion board; he figured out the "anonymous" poster's identity, and the offer was rescinded. How many of those "snarky" e-mail-exchanges- gone-viral have you received?

When you are networking online, just as when you are networking in person, start from a place where you can make a contribution. It is more valuable to participate or contribute thoughtfully to a discussion board in an area of your interest or expertise than it is to broadcast your name and résumé all over every job board. If you join a discussion board, "lurk" quietly until you get the feel of the environment. The protocols may not be obvious to a newbie, but they are often ruthlessly enforced. Refrain from flaming, even if it is tolerated; it can burn bridges and tarnish your reputation. And always be *very* careful and selective with e-mail jokes. They are an annoying interruption to many, and likely to be seen as in bad taste. It may seem like a small thing to you, but not to firms such as the one that summarily fired an employee who accidentally sent an off-color e-mail joke to the entire organization.

REDEFINING RAPPORT

Rapport isn't chemistry, and it isn't glad-handing. Rapport is the authentic networking tool that helps you keep in touch, share what you know, help others, and ask others for help. So, what can you do to increase your capacity to build rapport with the people you meet? Start with conversations, not small talk. Transactional networkers concentrate on what they will say and how to say it, but authentic networkers focus on how to listen and ask good questions. Then actively seek out new people and support the relationships you already have. Networking is *active*. When you're active—joining groups, attending meetings, calling members for no reason at all, offering advice—you're building rapport. Take the idea of give and take to heart. It is the foundation of strong relationships.

The idea of give and take is the foundation of strong relationships.

By building rapport, you make people feel comfortable and heard. You master the skill to start and guide a cordial conversation, whether it's sharing a few minutes of how-is-your-day-going stories over a cup of coffee or engaging in lengthy and complex business negotiations where everyone's opinions must be understood and respected. You develop rapport when you approach people as human beings, not as electronic transactions. It has been said that the most important trip you may ever take in life is meeting people halfway. Authentic networkers go beyond halfway to meet people wherever they find them.

Questions for Reflection

▷ Do you know at least two interesting personal facts about most of the people in your network?

▷ When attending an event or professional association meeting, what are some things you can do to be more at ease and make it easier to listen attentively to someone you have just met?

▷ How would you rate your rapport skills? What can you do to improve them?

▷ Can you think of a time you put someone in your network in the uncomfortable position of saying "no"? What do you wish you had done differently? Have you spoken to that person about the exchange?

REQUIREMENTS
What Matters Most

JULIA CALLED SUSAN, a professional acquaintance, to ask permission to use her name as a reference. Using classic networking rapport-building techniques, she first asked Susan about news in her life and brought her up-to-date on a volunteer project in which they both participated. Susan, however, seemed less than enthusiastic about helping Julia. What was the problem? Could it have been the nonstop "click, click" sounds that Susan could hear, telling her that Julia was "multitasking" at her computer even as she was asking for her friend's attention—and a favor? Was Susan wondering just how much Julia valued the relationship?

As a way of giving back to my network, I frequently offer coaching advice to friends of friends who are in transition. So, as a favor to a former colleague, I arranged to provide Tom with some career coaching by phone. Before our scheduled call, Tom did all the "mechanics" right: He sent me his résumé, outlined his job search concerns, and asked for thirty to forty minutes of my time. For the first five minutes of our conversation I kept hearing an annoying crunching noise in the background. "Are you eating?" I asked. "Well, yes," Tom replied, "I'm just finishing my breakfast," to which I said, "Well, either stop eating or let's stop talking!"

I don't know which bothered me more—that he was eating during our call, or that he was eating breakfast at 11:00 a.m.!

℘

Charles left George, a long-time member of his network, a message requesting advice on a business issue and asked for a call back by the end of the day. George carved out a moment and dialed Charles' number. "Oh, George—thanks for calling. Can I put you on hold for just a minute?" When he returned to the phone, Charles said, "Thanks for waiting. That was an important call." George felt insulted—after all, he was returning Charles' call. And wasn't *his* call important?

℘

You probably cringed while reading these true stories. I know I did when I wrote them.

At best, Julia, Tom, and Charles were clueless. Their conduct showed their lack of manners and respect for other people's time, expertise, and networks. This turned their everyday networking activities into displays of thoughtless or rude behavior. Not surprisingly, these events had a negative impact on the other party's desire to build relationships or speak highly of Julia, Tom, or Charles.

Are you thinking, "Have *I* ever acted that badly?" Probably, if you're human. Nobody sets out to be rude. Most of us work hard to live by the golden rules of courtesy and good manners we all were taught in school and at home. Yet when it comes to networking, most of us have been guilty of small acts of inconsiderate behavior, and we think we can get away with it.

There's nothing unique about networking courtesy; it calls on the same good manners we learned from our parents and teachers—but we sometimes forget manners and focus on mechanics when we are networking. Earlier in this book we learned that being aware of and taking responsibility for the way we act are at least as important as what we do. Earlier chapters on rapport and relationships offered examples of the spirit that animates authentic networking: reaching out to shake hands, smiling, and introducing yourself; remembering people's names and pronouncing them correctly; asking permission before using someone's name as a referral or a reference; being thoughtful and acting appropriately in every arena—in person, on the phone, and in writing. Even the "Wild West" of the Internet has rules of behavior.

Indeed, like everything else in life, networking has unwritten requirements and rules of the road. They are the starting points for creating success; ignoring them will set you up for failure. These unwritten rules are important to people and transgressions are always noticed. The "requirements" are where networking becomes practical, because every day we send public, real-world signals through our behaviors and activities. Respecting requirements means understanding that the manners of networking matter! So, it is worthwhile to look at the familiar networking mechanics. What is it that encourages people to want to know you, help you, and be part of your network?

This chapter introduces protocols and practices that are always top-of-mind for an authentic networker and explains how to put them into practice—every day. These go beyond the usual networking tips such as wear your name tag on your right side, hold your glass in your left hand, always introduce yourself, and so on. Those are the mechanics of networking. You will follow the "manners" of authentic networking when you redefine networking and bring a new spirit to those familiar activities: You adopt a welcoming attitude and offer a genuine smile, a cheerful and positive greeting, and a handshake. When you read a name tag you say the complete name, asking how to pronounce it if necessary, and use the name in the conversation. You take into account the feelings and comfort of others. You don't talk when the speaker is speaking. When you leave, you express appreciation for the time spent together and comment on something you learned.

Every day, and not just at professional events, authentic networkers adopt the practice of respecting other people's time and responsibilities; they are not just interested in others, they can put themselves in their shoes. When they meet someone—in person, on the phone or Internet, or through an organization—they know that etiquette, thoughtful behavior, and common sense matter.

THE PROTOCOLS OF NETWORKING

This chapter opened with stories of Julia, Tom, and Charles and their networking manners. What about your manners?

? Have you ever neglected to turn off your cell phone before entering a building or a meeting—because "it won't ring"?

▷ Have you ever been late, even a minute, to a meeting—because "they never start on time"?

▷ Have you ever texted while waiting for someone or during a meeting—because "no one will notice"?

▷ Have you ever sent an e-mail without checking it carefully (for correct formatting, grammar, spelling, tone, and attachments)—because you "need to get this out fast"?

▷ Have you ever left a rambling voice mail message that didn't include your name, reason for calling, and phone number in the first twenty seconds—because "it's just a quick phone call"?

If you have committed any of these transgressions, you may be paying more attention to the procedures and mechanics of networking than to the art of making a connection. You may have valued your own time and convenience more than the time and convenience of others. Infrequent faux pas will probably be forgotten or excused by members of your network with an "Oops, Patti must have been writing this e-mail at 5:30 a.m.; she forgot to send the attachment." But a pattern of missteps can limit your ability to network effectively and meet your goals. If you don't mind your networking manners or don't see them as important, people will remember you, but for all the wrong reasons. Remember: Your reputation consists of what people say about you. Its strength depends in part on whether gaffes are occasional and forgotten, or so common that they become part of your image and are passed on to others.

There's simply no excuse for not observing the courtesies of networking. Etiquette isn't old-fashioned; it is the timeless practice of building and strengthening relationships. It is hard to improve on the Bible's injunction to "Do unto others as you would have them do unto you," but many people have tried, formulating the rules of etiquette over the centuries. At sixteen,

George Washington penned a pamphlet called "Rules of Civility & Decent Behavior in Company and Conversation: A Book of Etiquette." In 1922, Emily Post published her famous volume of *Etiquette*, now in its seventeenth edition. Her great-grandson Peter Post, a syndicated columnist and writer, sums up the realm of business etiquette with three instructions: "Think before acting, make choices that build relationships, and do it sincerely." Etiquette isn't about everyone behaving exactly the same. We all come to networking from different starting points, and your personal approach is part of what makes your actions authentically "you." Of course, you need to be aware of and respect local standards of behavior and attire. But the spirit of good manners is essentially the same wherever you go. Here are some everyday, universal, real-world requirements.

Authentic networkers adopt a practice of respecting other people's time and responsibilities.

Be Punctual

The simple gesture of being on time is a fundamental rule of considerate behavior that will help you stand out from the crowd. Punctuality demonstrates that you respect other people's time and value it as much as your own. Arriving on time indicates your appreciation for and interest in the people you are scheduled to be with. Being on time means taking full responsibility, leaving plenty of time for traffic or train delays, and not blaming your GPS for directing you to the wrong place.

What happens if, despite your very best efforts, you keep someone waiting or are late for an appointment? Apologize briefly, explain why you were late, and ask whether she prefers to keep to what's left of the scheduled time or reschedule at her convenience. Don't waste her time with excuses. A quick "I'm very sorry to have kept you waiting, I misjudged morning traffic" is sufficient. Above all, don't blame your tardiness on anyone or anything other than yourself. Not long ago, I scheduled time to talk to a client about a job offer he was considering. After waiting ten minutes for his call, I called him. When he answered, he "apologized" by telling me he was busy packing for a trip. Then he offered the twenty-first century version of blaming the secretary: "I can't believe my BlackBerry didn't remind me it was time to call you."

Be Professional

Next, don't waste the time that others generously give you. People are juggling many priorities. The time they give you is time taken away from something or someone else, so after a courteous greeting, get to the point. For example, it is often convenient to deal with straightforward questions by phone or e-mail. This sounds simple and we do it all the time, but all too often one call or message turns into several, and a small request becomes a flood of interruptions. And too often we start these extra interruptions with wandering preambles: "Did you get my call? I meant to call you yesterday, but I've been busy." "I tried to reach you, but I got your voice mail and didn't want to leave a message." "I got your text, call me back." All that information is unnecessary; to the unlucky listener it seems to take forever before you get to the point so that she can give you what you need and return to the projects demanding her attention. My husband, a former business consultant (and now history professor who launched his second career through—you guessed it—networking), likes to say, "If you can't state what you need in the first two sentences, people will stop listening."

Follow Up and Follow Through

As any golfer will tell you, follow-through is what makes the difference between a good shot and a hike through the rough. Following through in the networking world means carrying out the next steps of your encounter and sharing the results. If you accept information, advice, or a referral from your network, it is your responsibility to use the gift and follow through on it in a timely manner. If someone suggests that you attend an event, attend. If someone suggests appropriate changes to the wording of your résumé, make the changes. If someone provides a referral, contact that person!

Once you've followed through, follow up! Get back to the person who helped you and inform him of the outcome. Following up is one of the most important, yet least practiced, protocols of networking. We all want to know how things turned out: Did you enjoy the event? Did you meet anyone I know? Was my advice helpful? Did the referral I made for you work out? Following up is a sign that you recognize and appreciate the other person's help, and it gives you an opportunity to ask, "Now, how can I help you?" When you don't follow through and follow up, you reinforce all of the negative stereotypes of networking. Following through effectively requires you to really listen to learn what other people are willing and able to do for you and to uncover opportunities to reciprocate or help them.

To follow up more effectively, I recommend creating a "Conversation Summary" after meetings and phone calls. Label it with the particulars of name, professional information, contact information, and purpose of the call. Then list both parties' follow-through action items and when you plan to follow up. This summary serves two purposes: It establishes a deadline

CONVERSATION SUMMARY
Name: Date:
Phone number: Connection:
Best e-mail address:
Reason for call:
Key knowledge acquired: *(insights, ideas, information, introductions)*
Action Item   Who Will Perform Action   When Due
IOU: How can I help you (or someone in your network)?

for you to complete your steps, and, if necessary, it acts as a cue to tactfully remind the other person of his or her deadline. Remember, people are usually willing to help, even though they have many priorities and your need may not be one of them. Your need will rate a higher priority for them if you follow through courteously.

Following up helps you avoid the number one mistake of networking: surprising people. No one likes to be surprised. When you follow up with people who have given you a name or a lead, it keeps them in the know. It lets them decide what—if anything—they want to do next. Let's say that I give you Mark's name. You call Mark and he agrees to meet with you. If you send me a brief text or e-mail telling me you have an appointment with Mark, I can thank him for seeing you and tell him more about you. If you don't follow through, when Mark says, "I saw your friend yesterday," all I can do is say, "Oh, thanks, did you?" Likewise, if you do a second follow-up call or e-mail to me after meeting with Mark, we can discuss what you learned. When I speak with him next, I may be able to reinforce your message or give him more information.

A Conversation Summary also helps you develop an "IOU list." By listening for how you can help as well as telling where you need help, you can discover problems you can help the other person solve, personal interests you can support by sending an article she may not have seen, or valuable introductions you can make to members of your network.

Say Thank You

This brings us to the most powerful follow-up: the thank you. Those two most meaningful words in networking are essential to making lasting connections. Showing genuine appreciation is simple, inexpensive, and tremendously effective. When you put those words in writing, *thank you* becomes even more powerful. Authentic networkers know the value of following up with a thank-you note, and they make sure their notes go well beyond the common "thank you for taking time from your busy day to meet with me" phrases. They check their Conversation Summaries and write about the insights they gained from the meeting or the outcomes of actions they took as a result of the conversation. That simple communication acknowledges what you learned and how it helped you. Even if you did not get the immediate results you hoped for, take the long-term view and thank them for what you learned; people appreciate your acknowledging the positive outcomes of the time they gave you.

Many books suggest that you write the note within twenty-four hours and that is generally good advice. But don't just rush back and fire off an e-mail follow-up or thank-you note. Sincerity is just as important as the timing of the note. Think about what you learned and consider why you are writing. Peter, a client, sent a thank-you note a full week after meeting with a referral. Faux pas? Maybe. But that note passed along useful information Peter had researched about the business and trends affecting his contact's business. It referred the recipient to a couple of articles and other resources that would help him with a current project. It also provided an update on how Peter had used information from their meeting.

Etiquette isn't old-fashioned; it is the timeless practice of building and strengthening relationships.

So, the note had meaning and muscle and conveyed more than just thanks for the minutes they had spent together. Like Peter, there may be times when you want to take a few days to collect information that will be useful to the other person. And although an e-mail is as appropriate a means of writing a thank you as "snail mail," be sure to use the *receiver's* preferred format, not the one that is easy or convenient for you. Consider sending a handwritten thank you; it is more valuable and lasting than any e-mail when it's done well. It's memorable because it is personal. It shows that you value the exchange enough to take the time and thought necessary to actually write a note. After all, you can't copy and paste pen and ink—yet!

Don't limit your efforts to thanking people for interviews, referrals, and other obvious career management gestures. Keep your eyes open for opportunities to express your appreciation on a regular basis. When someone offers a suggestion, thank her even if you choose not to take the advice; her opinion of you as a person who is willing to do things differently is a positive statement about you. On the other hand, send a note of acknowledgment when someone follows your advice: "I'm happy to know my suggestions helped." When someone gives you a compliment or refers your services, take a few minutes to thank him and promise to keep him posted on any developments. If you pitch a great idea but your supervisor or client turns you down, thanking that person for her time and honesty leaves the situation on a positive note and keeps the door open for future interactions. When a co-worker helps on a project, give thanks and credit where it is due. And every time you land a job, send a thank-you note to everyone who helped you along the way. Yes, everyone.

Your Business Card: Don't Leave Home without It

Just as our Victorian ancestors used the subtle language of the calling card to express ultimate courtesy, you can use your business card to demonstrate good networking manners. You may think a business card is a pretty minor detail today—hey, you're on Facebook and LinkedIn. But your business card is a must-have accessory of your work life no matter what your age or field. Think of it as a handshake you leave behind—a professional, tangible way for each person to remember the other. Make sure that memory is a positive one by following these best-practice protocols.

Punctuality demonstrates that you value other people's time as much as your own.

Business cards are designed to be exchanged. Always carry a couple of them with you (put your cards in your right-hand pocket and collect other people's cards in your left-hand pocket). Give your card in a way that will encourage people to remember you and get in touch with you. For example, say something about what's on your card and what you do. In Japan, business cards are exchanged with bows and are attentively and respectfully read. This full ceremonial approach might be over the top in your country, but the spirit is right. So, when you receive a card, take a second to look at it and find something positive to say about it. "Oh, is this a new company?" or "That's a striking company logo!" or "VP of Technology—that must be a constantly changing job."

And when you receive a business card, don't just file it away. Turn it over and jot down whatever you know about the person—hobbies, interests, children—that might be helpful in later conversations.

Finally, never force your cards on people. Share them with courtesy and discretion. Sometimes it's best to wait until they are asked for. And please don't pass your business cards out at social occasions, as one guest actually did at my holiday party!

Persevere

Perseverance is a networking necessity. It's most frequently seen in the way a networker reaches out to people from whom he or she would like to receive help. There is a right way and a wrong way to persevere. The right way is *persistence*. When I was just starting my consulting practice, I responded to a Request for Proposals at a large local firm. As is often the case, nothing happened. A few weeks later, I left the contact person a cordial voice mail message offering to provide whatever additional information she might need. Every three to four weeks for the next six months, I called and left a very brief, upbeat message stating my continued interest and availability. One day I got a call from the company's head of HR. "Some management changes have delayed this project, but now we'd like to move forward. Of all the people who submitted proposals, you were the only one who kept in touch in a positive way. Will you come in next Wednesday to discuss the project?" That consulting assignment lasted three years, and the friendships that formed as a result continue to this day.

On the other hand, a person can persevere to the point of becoming a *pest*. After a talk I gave on the struggles of connecting with key professionals during a job hunt, a man—let's call him "Frank"—stood up and asked what he could have done differently. Frank wanted a job in accounting. He reached an insider at his target company and got a referral to the hiring director, whom he called. The hiring director said, "I'm busy right now; call me back after budget season. I'm swamped until October." But the job was open, and Frank didn't want to be overlooked during the job inter-

The two most meaningful words in networking: thank you.

viewing process that he presumed was going on *now*. So, he called the hiring director not once, but several times over the course of the next few weeks, leaving messages about his "fit" for the job and asking if interviews had started. The director never called back, and Frank never got the chance to be interviewed. His question: Why didn't his persistence pay off? A member of the audience shouted out, "You weren't being persistent, you were being a pest! The guy *told* you he was busy for the next two months."

These two stories demonstrate the difference between persevering and being a pest. People will remember you—and avoid you—if you annoy them.

Perseverance means patience and reaching out in ways that strengthen your relationships. Instead of responding with impatience ("I'm tired of waiting—I'm going to call today even though she asked me to call next week," or "I made the call but she hasn't called me back"), persevere in an appropriate way. Respect the schedules and convenience of others. Keep your calls upbeat and don't leave a voice mail every single time you call. Of course, keep calling; it is your responsibility to make the connection. But authentic networkers know that no one wants a box full of e-mails or voice mails with the same message from one person. People know you want to talk—but they may just be too busy at the moment, or for the next month! Instead of pestering, leave a clear, straightforward message about your reason for calling, tell them you will try again in a few days, and let them know how best to reach you if they have time. On the second and third calls, hang up if the person does not answer. On the fourth try, leave an upbeat message to the effect that you hope the two of you can speak soon. Finally, if you never get through, call the person's assistant and ask if there is a better time or way to make the connection. Never, ever say, "You haven't called me back." Follow a similar process with e-mail. Your first e-mail should be succinct and straightforward, and something the receiver can pass on to someone else for action. If you don't get a response, try again three or four days later, then pick up the phone.

Authentic networkers try to put themselves in the other person's shoes.

Persistence doesn't guarantee success. Sooner or later, your networking efforts will be rejected. Respect "no" and move on without complaining, blaming, or asking why. Asking why serves nothing; it is intrusive and guilt-inducing. "No" is not a rejection of you, but the way you accept "no" can cause you to be rejected later! If you are realistic in your expectations, rejection is about *their* time, *their* network, and *their* needs. It is not about you unless you have a reputation for asking for too much or acting inappropriately.

Be Prepared

Another way to act professionally is to prepare, as the Boy Scouts have been advising for more than a hundred years. Things can get out of hand very quickly when you're networking. You're meeting people, making and checking in with connections, and finding ways to offer and give help. With all of that going on, it's easy to get overwhelmed and shift into short-term thinking, allowing follow-up and follow-through to fall through the cracks. Authentic networking is based on long-term thinking, as we've discussed throughout this book, and a key to long-term success is preparation.

Being prepared begins with planning. Planning every meeting, scripting cold calls, even thinking what you would say if you ran into someone on the street, isn't being phony. On the contrary, thinking ahead to how an interaction might play out will make you more confident and comfortable in the moment. Doing research can help you anticipate obstacles and avoid being surprised by tricky questions. Ask yourself "What could go wrong?" and have a plan to deal with that possibility.

MIND YOUR P'S AND Q'S

Creating, building, sustaining, maintaining, and expanding your network requires energy and effort every day of your life. The bottom line is that authentic networkers make that effort and try to put themselves in the other person's shoes. This basic etiquette will help you build rapport and develop the relationships that can support a network to last a lifetime.

Questions for Reflection

▷ Can you think of an instance when someone showed that he or she did not value your time? How did that make you feel?

▷ When was the last time you kept someone waiting for an appointment or did not promptly return an e-mail or phone call? Did you apologize? How?

▷ What is your method of keeping track of follow-up and follow-through tasks?

▷ When was the last time you wrote a thank-you note? When did you last receive one?

▷ Think of three people in your network. How do they prefer to be contacted? If you don't know, how can you find out?

RESEARCH
Life Is a Learning Experience

YOU MAY WONDER WHY a book about networking includes an entire chapter on research. After all, research is a solitary, heads-down, what-do-I-need-to-know-to-write-that-paper-or-back-up-my-report activity, right? Wrong! When you redefine research, you'll find it's much more interesting than just hitting the books and gathering facts. That's because, while money used to make the world go round, knowledge is what makes it spin today. Everyone knows that "Knowledge is power." Bill Gates took that view a step further when he said, "Power comes not from knowledge kept, but from knowledge shared." Gates was confirming a basic principle of knowledge management, a discipline that has transformed many organizations over the past twenty years. Knowledge management aims to elicit and share the experiences and intelligence of everyone working on a project or in an organization so that information and intellectual assets can be transformed into enduring value. Many organizations have formal knowledge management initiatives, with written protocols, complex programs, and computer systems to back them up. But you can reap the benefits of this approach informally in your everyday life too.

Knowledge is not only fundamental to organizational success, it is also a key networking building block. Authentic networkers know that; they invest in research for the long term because they understand the value of knowledge in developing reputations, building rapport, and strengthening relationships. This lesson explains how research can build your knowledge base for success, and then shows the role it plays in the powerful give-and-take of networking and personal enrichment.

BECOMING A STUDENT

Being ready is the secret of success. It's the competitive advantage. As baseball great Ted Williams said, "You've got to be ready for the fastball." Champion football coach Bear Bryant's winning philosophy also relied on readiness: "Expect the unexpected." These two talented and highly successful students of their sports never stopped thinking and learning about the game; each was always looking for ways to improve his skills and his team's performance. There are many talented people in this world, but the truly successful ones have something in common: They are lifelong students of their respective games. What are you a student of? Do you take responsibility for pursuing your interests and learning more? Research can transform you from a person with a little knowledge (or a lot of miscellaneous knowledge) into a star performer within your profession or field. Research helps us test our thinking, check our attitudes, and discover whether our information is correct or flawed. It's a way to learn about people, anticipate problems, and analyze results. It's a way to build new knowledge and skills that will benefit us and the members of our networks.

Although research is all about doing your homework and being prepared, being prepared today means more than lining up facts and information and doing due diligence so that you can answer difficult questions. For authentic networkers, research is a means of exercising intellectual curiosity, a quest for ideas, expertise, and innovation that is not limited to formal inquiry or investigation. Authentic networkers are curious and *interested*,

Money used to make the world go round, but knowledge is what makes it spin today.

either by temperament or by training. They understand that while much depends on what they know, even more depends on what they can learn. They also want to benefit others in their network by sharing what they know. So, they view research as a creative activity that keeps their curiosity alive and improves their ability to think outside the box. Whether by reading business journals and local newspapers to see what's going on, or staying abreast of important trends, research is their way of staying engaged in the changing world around them.

THE BENEFITS OF "NEW-FASHIONED" RESEARCH

Most people know how to use traditional research methods to sharpen the tools of old-style mechanical networking. Spending an afternoon on the Internet or in the library will let you tailor your résumé and cover letter to a targeted company or position. A quick Google search will yield personal and professional information as you prepare for an interview. These standard research tools help us answer questions about people, companies, industries, and the world at large. Authentic networkers, however, lift the concept of research from this transactional, short-term level to the longer-term context of relationship building and knowledge sharing. Viewed through a long-term lens, research is about investing in yourself by learning, sharing, and serving others. Research is an easy give-and-take networking tool: The more research you do, the more knowledge you can give to others and the more knowledge you will receive in return.

Research can also help you build your network. A little research will help you find the right person to talk to for almost any situation. By tapping your network, you can reach out and meet with people you don't know personally. (This process can be made simpler if people you know use LinkedIn or other social networking tools that identify people they know or provide paths to people in specific companies.)

Finally, because research reflects not only curiosity but also effort and enthusiasm, it is a good first step for any networking activity. One of our networking principles is that networking doesn't just happen; a network is earned through thoughtful effort. In building relationships, visible effort and enthusiasm will help you strengthen the connections in your network. The preparation you put into getting to know someone and having a productive and mutually beneficial meeting lets this person know that she is important to you. Studying a topic with the other person's point of view in mind helps build rapport; it creates a basis for meaningful discussion on topics that matter to your network partners. Or, as one of my clients summed it up in her formula for success, "I know what they need before I introduce myself to them." Researching in this new-fashioned way achieves that goal and shows consideration, a courtesy that is one of the requirements of authentic networking. It helps you talk their language rather than appear uninformed or, worse, arrogant or uncaring.

THE ART OF RESEARCH

Whether you are working in a scientific laboratory, studying in a library, or enjoying coffee with a friend, research is the art of asking good questions and then following up with more good questions. By posing questions and getting feedback, you gather information, clarify what you've heard, enlarge upon the subject, or go into more depth on a particular topic. Doing your research is about asking smart questions and listening intently, and then taking responsibility to follow the trail wherever it leads you—to the Internet, to a bookstore, or to people who can help you (usually people who have faced the same issue themselves).

You'll feel more comfortable with the idea of research when you expand your notion of what it is. In the most general sense, you are researching whenever you attend a seminar, listen to a speaker, or read a book; when you study a company's printed materials or pursue general career advice. You are even conducting research when browsing through book summaries on Amazon.com to get an idea of important topics in a field. Have you taken an overview course lately, or attended a seminar or a conference? Or attended events that were "off the beaten path" for you? All of this is research. All are excellent ways to learn more about the world at large or a topic that interests you. Experiences such as these will sharpen your skills and give you opportunities to make new connections in your profession.

? How have you learned more about a company or industry that interests you?

▷ Who have you tapped your in your network for more information?

▷ What else can you do to increase your knowledge?

For some people, pursuing an advanced degree or certificate is an important but daunting avenue of research. One of my clients felt his lack of a college degree held him back from promotion opportunities. When I asked him why he hadn't returned to school, he answered, "I'll be thirty-nine before I finish." Guess what. You're going to be thirty-nine whether you go back to school or not.

Just as questions are key research tools, so is listening. How you listen matters as much as what you ask. Good listeners are incredibly curious and want to know *why* and *how*. Look back at the different kinds of questions we discussed in the Rapport lesson. Skip yes/no questions, and avoid "recital" questions—those for which the person probably has prepared or even rehearsed an answer. You will learn no more than you would by reading a press release. Instead, ask questions that address deeper knowledge: How did you decide to do this? Who else has done this? What will be the impact? What will it change?

Authentic networkers understand the value of knowledge in developing reputations, building rapport, and strengthening relationships.

How did you do that? What else can you tell us? Questions such as these show you have taken responsibility and are serious about your research; they demonstrate you have prepared. Asking them acknowledges there is more to tell or learn.

Only a few people are wise enough to benefit from one kind of research: learning from experience—yours and others'. If you take responsibility for your actions, you can learn from your mistakes—turn them into reference points as my client Stuart advised—and use them to make course corrections. Learning from mistakes doesn't mean blaming yourself; it means accepting yourself and recognizing that your actions have consequences, and then analyzing the consequences and adjusting your actions accordingly.

Unfortunately, although many people attend the School of Hard Knocks, few of them graduate! This is another great reason to have a network. Your network can help you make fewer mistakes, either by providing timely feedback or by sharing the lessons that others have learned through experience. And when mistakes do happen—as we know they will—your network is there to offer support and a guiding hand that can put you back on the right track.

TOOLS FOR SUCCESSFUL RESEARCH

The preliminary research (what I like to call the "quiet phase" of research) demonstrates courtesy. When you find out everything you can on your own, before talking with your network, you show respect by not asking people to waste their time filling you in on things you should know or can learn on your own. People want to help, but they want to help someone who has already taken the first steps, who knows and can articulate what he or she needs. Preliminary research opens the door to more interesting in-depth conversations and helps you find something you can offer in return. This turns your conversation from *asking*—for answers or favors—to *sharing* or *exchanging* ideas and information.

Today, the Internet is the obvious first stop for basic information on people, organizations, and industries. Start with a Google search, and then dive into company Web sites for information on organizational history, management, products, and services. Read deeper on the search results page for other points of view, both positive and negative, including news articles, press releases, customer blogs, product or service reviews, opportunities, and problems.

Web sites are great, but never underestimate the usefulness of public data, much of which is available through your public library. Hoover's Online assembles information on public companies, including summaries of operations, financial data, management teams, directors, and news stories. Check out Dun & Bradstreet's Million Dollar Directory and Ward's Business Directory. If a company isn't listed in standard reference books, it's typically because it's small, new, or listed by an acronym instead of its full legal name. Your librarian may be able to help. Of course, public companies are the easiest to research because they are required to file annual reports and financial documents. But even privately held companies have Web sites and publications, belong to trade associations, or are featured in news articles or documents that you can find through LexisNexis. They have competitors and relationships with suppliers or fellow professionals that you can explore through your best tool: your network.

? You can learn many facts about people and organizations on the Internet.
Take a moment to do some research on an individual—yourself or someone you know.

  ▷ What can you learn about an individual through Google?
  ▷ What can you learn through LinkedIn?
  ▷ What other sites can you use?

No one has access to all the information that's out there. That's why, beyond standard research, you need a network of knowledgeable people—including competitors, customers, current and former employees, and vendors
of the companies you are targeting. Authentic networkers know that once
they have completed their preliminary research and learned all they can on
their own, their best resource is their network. It can provide more in-depth
information and the "inside scoop" you will not find elsewhere. Take a moment and go back to your Worlds I Travel In worksheet (page 48). Who in
your network can help you? What type of knowledge can you gather from
your networking world?

When you talk with members of your network, take advantage of the
nuances that only in-person conversations with real people can provide.
Listen for themes as much as details. Do people talk about the products or
about the culture and the team? Look for recurring patterns: If one topic
keeps popping up, dig deeper into that topic with thoughtful follow-up
questions.

Some people turn to online communities for background information
on companies. *Fast Company* reported on one woman who wanted to
change jobs, but didn't know how her skills would transfer. She needed to
network, and fast. She didn't hit the party circuit, attend career fairs, or
search the classifieds. Instead, she joined the
e-mail section for the Silicon Valley Chapter of Webgrrls International, an online and
offline network focused on advancing the careers of women. "I instantly had
access to more than 1,000 people," she said. "The list is my virtual Rolodex."
She used that network to tap into available jobs, and then to get advice when
an offer came through. Other members shared their opinions about the pros
and cons of working for the company.

What are you a student of?

RESEARCH DURING TRANSITIONS

A client told me that one of the most important things he learned during his transition was recognizing how little he really knew. This realization is the first step toward taking responsibility for what you must do. This advertisement for an investment service sums up the challenge: "What do you know? What don't you know? How do you propose to find out?" Perhaps because we discover in transitions a gap between what we know and what we need to know, research is especially valuable during these periods. Transitions are a frequent topic in this book, and this lesson on research is a good place to look especially closely at how one aspect of networking plays out during this particular phase of our lives.

> *Research is the art of asking good questions and then following up with more good questions.*

If you are in a transition, you will want to focus your research by studying your target industry. Taking a course in your target field might be appropriate. Professional conferences can be useful if you attend them with a purpose in mind. Do you want to meet new people? Process new ideas? Ask, "What will I learn and whom will I meet?" And before you go, conduct some pre-research: Review the materials, visit the conference Web site, call the organizers, and check your word-of-mouth network. Learn whether people who have attended this conference in the past speak well of it.

While you are in a career change or job search, your research will include looking at several different employers and developing a standard list of questions, the answers to which can amount to comparative snapshots. Which are the industry's key firms and rising challengers? How big are these firms? Who are their primary competitors? What is their global reach? Are their technologies on the way in or on the way out? Directories, online databases, and annual reports can guide you. Business and trade journals can be full of useful information on executive changes and strategic initiatives. Approach these resources as a student, not as a job seeker, and you will learn more.

Once you target a particular organization, narrow your research focus and dig even deeper. Use the company Web site to contact investor relations departments, which will send information on request. Most PR sites archive press releases, which make for good background reading. Study the annual reports and check reference books for correct names, titles, and addresses.

Drilling still deeper, visit the company's local office to get a feel for the organization. Use its product or talk to someone who uses its services. If you have an appointment, arrive twenty to thirty minutes early to cast a last-minute look around. Most important, learn about the inner workings of the organization. Every organization has a unique culture and its own ways of thinking and doing things. Even in the context of shared economic or market conditions, each has its own concerns and goals. Look at these in the context of the next eighteen to twenty-four months and think about what your skills and abilities could contribute. How can you help this company achieve its goals?

You can find the "hard" data online or in published sources, but the best way to research the important "soft" data—on organizational culture, attitudes, and the styles of key individuals—is to tap your network. People in your network, and others in their networks, can provide insiders' perspectives on a company's reputation and culture, and the direction the industry is moving. You won't get this in print sources. The same network contacts can provide insights into the individuals you hope to meet. It's always helpful to know the personal and professional backgrounds of the people who run the company you want to join. Your network will supplement what you learn through public sources and bring it up-to-date. What is her job title? What are his responsibilities? What is her background? What are his interests and hobbies? After you come up with some facts, your network may be able to fill in the blanks.

If you are meeting with someone for the first time, what you learn through research can help you break the ice and build rapport to get the conversation off to a good start. The fact that you have done your research will be apparent, earning you credibility. The knowledge you bring lets you ask the right questions at the right time and alerts you to "danger zones" and topics to avoid. So, before you set up an appointment, use the wide variety of research tools and networking connections you have. Go in prepared with knowledge you can share, or don't go in at all.

And don't forget that the person you meet with has probably researched *you*! One businesswoman I know spent weeks setting up an important sales appointment with a senior executive in another city. When she arrived in his office, his first question was "Why should I be talking to you? I Googled you and couldn't find anything about you—no accomplishments, no publications." Ouch!

RAMPING UP RESEARCH

Authentic networkers don't see research as "homework"; rather, they understand that research pays big dividends. When you are just starting out in your career or taking a new direction, research will help you refine your choices and learn the ropes. Studying an industry or profession will let you determine if it is right for you before you commit to it long-term. Then you can delve deeper into any companies that interest you to get a feel for the atmosphere and culture as well as the actual work involved. Volunteer stints, internships, and part-time jobs are excellent ways to see a field or organization from the inside. When financier Charles Schwab was a young student, he held jobs at an insurance

Turn your mistakes into reference points.

company, a bank, and a financial services firm. "I worked after school," he remembers, "on weekends and during the summers. They were a lot of junk jobs, but I made it a point to really understand the mechanics of the financial-services world." Another payoff of research when you are starting out is that it instantly increases your credibility. Many applicants walk into job interviews with no more than a résumé and a smile, but if you've done your research, people will see you are focused and interested in their organization. Learn something about the business, their competitors, and major trends in the industry. There is one question an interviewer almost always asks: "Why do you want to work here?" Research lets you skip the generic answers—"It's a good opportunity, a short commute, an excellent place to learn . . ." and move into more substantive topics.

Good research means you can answer the second most important question of any interview: "What do you know about us?" One interviewer told a client, "I've seen your impressive résumé and feel that I know a lot about you. What do you want to know about us?" That really shifted the conversation. Luckily my client had done her research and easily came up with smart questions. She had developed a framework about that organization's needs, the needs of the position, and the interviewer's needs and she connected how her skills and interests aligned with those needs.

It's well known that the vast majority of positions are not filled through advertising, job boards, or even search firms; they are filled through word of mouth, so your network is the best place to look for leads. Once you locate a suitable position, go on a fact-finding mission. Touch base with the data providers in your network—the people who can give you good, solid information—and get your facts in order before you make a call to the decision maker or the door opener. Their knowledge is your best research.

What questions should you ask if a member of your network gives you a referral to a person who may be able to help you? For some, it would be, "Can you give me his title, e-mail, and phone number?" Authentic networkers would ask, "Can you share how you know this person? When was the last time you spoke or met? How do you think he can help me and how can I help him?" This is on-the-spot research that can warm up what could otherwise feel too much like a cold call.

Research turns your conversation from asking to sharing or exchanging.

If your connection gives you more than one name, continue your research with this question: "Thanks for the names. If you were me, who would you call first?" Your connection may reply, "Well, I gave you three names, but you know what? Call Joe first, not this other guy. I know Joe and he does . . ." Then ask, "How do you know Joe?" It matters whether they sat together at a breakfast meeting or they have known each other for fifteen years! Next, ask, "How do you think Joe can help me?" Then ask the most important question: *"How can I help Joe?"* When you speak with Joe, you want a meeting of equals; you want Joe to see you as a potential resource, someone he would like to add to his network.

When you pursue a particular position, research will help you mold your résumé and cover letter. Generic letters often end up in the wastebasket; make your letter show you understand the company's business and the challenges it faces, and address ways you can help the company. Your research can start with something as simple as using the company's product or service to provide a bridge to your knowledge and expertise. The more you understand the business challenges facing a potential employer, the less important your limited experience in a particular industry can be.

Once you land an interview, research is one form of preparation that will help you build confidence. The reason is simple: The best way to alleviate the natural fear of the unknown is to learn more about the situation. Many people feel anxious in an interview or other one-on-one situation. After all, if you haven't done your homework up front, you'll be shut down by an unexpected question. Confidence is in the details. If your research is thorough, you will relax and feel more comfortable. You will be able to ask intelligent questions, demonstrating your knowledge along with your expertise and experience.

It's impossible to anticipate every question, but the better prepared you are for an interview, the better you will perform. Your preparation should include anticipating who you will be speaking with, what questions they are likely to ask, and why they will ask them. Your network can provide advance insights about the people you will meet, so you can be mentally prepared and have information ready to formulate responses that will reinforce your message.

Some people will try to put you on the spot to test your nerves, show off their own knowledge, or impress others in the room. If someone asks you something you don't know the answer to, never, ever try to bluff your way through. People can tell if you don't know what you're talking about. The best answer is an honest one. Simply say, "I don't know the answer to that question. I will find out and get back to you quickly." Then make sure you follow up. As we have learned, follow-ups are an excellent opportunity to strengthen the connection and get your message out a second time.

LIFELONG LEARNING

Like networking, research isn't just about getting a job. The same research skills that you put to use professionally can help you meet your personal goals. A Boston woman had always dreamed of dancing with the Rockettes in New York City. Although she was a trained and enthusiastic dancer, her career path and work life went in an entirely different direction. During the Q&A session of a mid-career development conference, she stood up in front of 500 attendees and asked, "I've always wanted to be a Rockette. Isn't it too late?" About 497 people started to laugh. Then another attendee stood up and shared that she knew someone who had been a Rockette and that the Rockettes alumni association invites other talented dancers to join them for local variety and charity shows. By finding time in her busy work life to attend this conference and having the courage to stand up and ask for help, she "tapped" into a new network and completed the research she needed to fulfill a lifelong dream.

THE PERSONAL PAYOFFS OF RESEARCH

As the expression of your intellectual curiosity, research can be the "fun" part of networking, if you see networking as a discovery process and view every day as an opportunity to learn something new. Your research activities link all your interests, from the books at your bedside to the challenges your industry faces in the next five years. They span the diverse range of people in your network and connect what you talk about with each one of them. Authentic networkers are naturally curious and open to exploring the unknown and the unexpected. Act as a learner, not as a knower. Be a lifelong student and respond to any situation with an open mind and a desire to learn. Read widely. Be aware of what people around you are thinking. Share your knowledge so that it becomes a valuable asset to you and others. Understand the substantive issues as well as the politics and personalities. While you will never have all the data you need to go forward without risk, research can make the difference between a good decision and a good guess.

Be a lifelong student and respond to any situation with an open mind and a desire to learn.

Questions for Reflection

▷ What are you a student of? What are you curious about learning?

▷ Do you routinely Google people before meeting with them?

▷ What was the last topic you researched in the library or online?

▷ What are three ways (besides the Internet) that you can learn something about a company's product or service?

REACHING OUT
Coming Full Circle

HARRIET WAS AT A CROSSROADS; she needed some serious career advice before making a decision. She turned to Evelyn, an executive who had always been her role model, even though the two women did not have a close relationship. Evelyn listened carefully, and then she shared some stories from her own career that gave Harriet a new perspective on her problem.

Harriet made her choice and, over time, she achieved great success in her profession. Years later, one thing bothered her about that conversation: She had never really thanked Evelyn for her candor and advice, and she didn't see a way to thank her now. Then, one afternoon, Harriet looked up from her desk to see Stanley, anxiously twisting his papers and asking to speak privately with her. As she talked with Stanley, Harriet understood that she could express her gratitude to Evelyn by helping someone else.

This final lesson focuses on one of the most satisfying parts of professional and personal success: reaching out to give or share with others. Reaching out brings your networking efforts full circle. I call the process of making your time, knowledge, and connections available to others "becoming a resource." When you become a resource to others, you simultaneously give and receive benefit. Your relationships become stronger, building rapport becomes easier, and your reputation is enhanced. Paradoxical as it may seem, the reward for taking responsibility, managing your career, fulfilling the requirements of authentic networking, and doing your research is that you are given the opportunity to give.

You reach out and become a resource because you understand that, in the long run, "what goes around comes around." In networking, a lot of "going around" may happen before it comes around—that meeting in August may produce a call in November. By now, it should be no surprise that networking is more an art than a science. It is exchanging without keeping score. It is a natural way to make a difference and have a lasting impact. Its effects are not easy to quantify by title, corner office, or compensation, yet they are powerful nonetheless. Networkers make the business world go round by reaching out to others.

BECOME A RESOURCE

Your network is built on three important building blocks: genuineness, courtesy, and reciprocity. Unlike people who put off working on their networks until the day they need them, authentic networkers use genuineness, courtesy, and reciprocity every day to build a reserve that's ready when they want it. Their definition of networking isn't asking for help; it's about helping others along the way. After all, whether people are reaching out to help you or you are reaching out to help them, it's all the same if you have built a network based on the lessons in this book.

Authentic networking is not for everyone. It's not for the person who, when I asked her for her thoughts on networking, said, "If there's no business to be had from knowing you, there's no reason to know you." It's not for the person who believes that making a certain number of phone calls each day is the way to get a job, or who likes to drop names about who is in his network. Transactional networkers measure results in business cards collected, referrals garnered, or contacts "linked in." Authentic networkers may have some of the same objectives, but they judge themselves successful when they are seen as a resource. They know that when they help someone who has a question or wants feedback, advice, or referrals, they earn that person's respect. They know that if they want to go to the top of the list of people known for having valuable thoughts and opinions,

Reaching out brings your networking efforts full circle.

they must share their thoughts and opinions freely and, if they don't have the answer, find someone who does.

In becoming a resource, you see yourself as a steward of your time and talent, and you become part of the solution process. You earn a reputation as someone who "has something to give that people can use," as one of my clients described a colleague. One benefit of earning this reputation is that it allows you to drop by without an appointment or gets you quick responses to your e-mails. I recently received a message from a resource in my network with the subject line "Need Advice." I clicked it open right away.

Authentic networkers use genuineness, courtesy, and reciprocity every day to build a reserve that's ready when they want it.

In order to bring your networking full circle, you must build the bridge between being helped and helping others. Belonging to a network doesn't mean you are an entry on a list of names and numbers; it means you participate in a web of mutual obligations, willingly undertaken and repaid, and based on the principle of reciprocity.

THE RECIPROCITY PRINCIPLE

Psychologists have identified reciprocity as a basic human behavioral norm. Human beings want—even need—to give something in return when they receive something of value. This principle pervades all our interactions, including routine exchanges with strangers. Even the simplest "Thank you" is followed by the reciprocal gesture of "You're welcome."

The reciprocity principle has several interesting features. First, the gift must be of value to the recipient. To offer something of real value, you must drop your own agenda and listen with care, ask "What does this person need?" and then offer to do what you do best. When you know your strengths, and let others know what they are, then you can share them regularly in work and life activities. You can respond with something that the other person will value.

A second fact about reciprocity is that the urge to reciprocate is strongest when the gift is given with no expectation of anything in return. This is the great paradox of reciprocity and of everday networking: Give without expectations of anything in return and you will reap great rewards. Authentic networkers learn early on that the more they give, the more they get back.

Paying It Forward

The desire to reciprocate is strong even when it isn't possible to repay the giver. A young man once asked Bernard Meltzer, a longtime radio personality and advice columnist, how he could repay an elderly uncle's generosity. Meltzer suggested he approach it in this way: "Tell him, 'I don't know when or how I can pay you back.' You may never pay the person back. However, there will come a time in future years when you will be successful. Someone will come to you for help. You must leave the door open. You must listen and you must try to be of assistance, and then you can say, 'I'm paying back Uncle Joe.' "

Sociologists call the concept of discharging a debt by paying someone other than the original benefactor *generalized reciprocity* or *generalized exchange*. When you cannot pay a person *back* for his or her help, you must instead pay it *forward* by helping a different person. This idea of paying it forward has been popular in recent years and was even the subject of a movie. But it isn't new; it was the subject of a Greek play written in 317 BC and Benjamin Franklin evoked the same idea in a letter written in 1784:

> "I do not pretend to give such a Sum; I only lend it to you. When you [...] meet with another honest Man in similar Distress, you must pay me by lending this Sum to him; enjoining him to discharge the Debt by a like operation, when he shall be able, and shall meet with another opportunity. I hope it may thus go thro' many hands, before it meets with a Knave that will stop its Progress. This is a trick of mine for doing a deal of good with a little money."

Ralph Waldo Emerson echoed the idea in his essay, "Compensation": "In the order of nature we cannot render benefits to those from whom we receive them, or only seldom. But the benefit we receive must be rendered again, line for line, deed for deed, cent for cent, to somebody."

It's not about keeping score. Authentic networkers know that they are indebted to countless others for innumerable large and small acts of kindness and assistance. If they were keeping strict accounts, they would never be able to repay them all. So, when you appreciate what someone has given you, your responsibility is to either pay it back or pay it forward, beyond a simple thank-you note. As one valued member of my network puts it, "I will be able to help that person on the spot or sometime later, or I'll be able to help someone else in the same or better way." Strive to add value to every connection you make and to contribute at least as much as—if not more than—you take away.

HOW TO REACH OUT

When was the last time you offered your ideas to a colleague? In the past year, have you volunteered to participate in an organization-wide team or task force? When an out-of-work acquaintance phones, do you take the call? Do you look for ways to save time for others? The answers to these questions suggest how much you reach out to others, or how you respond when others ask you for feedback, advice, or referrals. It's not only your knowledge that draws people to you; the way you signal your availability through building rapport, listening, and communicating is just as important. You can't share knowledge if people are afraid to talk with you or are unwilling to keep you posted on what's going on. The way you respond when people ask you for help is a key factor in whether you are added to their networks and whether you become top-of-mind when they are looking for input. And when they ask, answer in a positive way using clear language. Make your advice or support specific, to the point, and objective. Use "can-do" language: "I'll find out." "What I can do is . . ." "I'll try my best." "I will get back to you." "Here's what you need to know." "Here's who you can call."

For many, the first step in becoming a resource is recognizing that you *can* help others by giving, sharing, or teaching. Perhaps you are just starting out and feel that you have little to offer, or you are in transition and feel ill-equipped to help. Just remember, we all have the ability to do something for others. What skills, knowledge, or expertise are you known for? You can advise, coach, coordinate, develop, deliver, facilitate, implement, recruit, write, create, attend, edit, teach, join, contact, refer. It's as simple as "I thought this might interest you." "Why don't you come with me to the professional association I belong to?" "Be my guest." Think of how you can be there for someone else, either professionally or personally.

Going the extra mile can take different forms—from making that amazing introduction to just taking the time to really listen. It doesn't have to be a big thing like a formal mentoring relationship. In fact, you may be surprised how much others appreciate small gestures. Once, when I was leading a team-building workshop for new employees of a large organization, I encouraged them to help one another. One woman replied, "How can I help anyone? I just started, and I don't know anything!" A young man quickly corrected her. "That's not so! During lunch today you explained the subway system to me; that will probably save me twenty minutes a day!" So, get over the feeling that you have nothing to offer.

Still wondering how you can become a resource to others? Look back at your signature line (in the Reputation lesson). Your signature line tells people where you can help. In my network, I'm called a networking guru—not for all the people I know, but for my ability to help people build their networks by being themselves and by identifying everyday ways they can give and so receive. My signature line reminds me and others of one way that I can be of service. Your signature line highlights your special gifts in the same way.

? In what ways can you be a resource to others in your network?

What is your signature line?

What does your signature line tell others about how you can help?

To be a true resource, however, you have to open your door. Your signature line helps make you visible, but to be of value to others you must be *available*. Being a resource means you are available to assist as well as to be assisted. It's taking people's phone calls, listening, and asking good questions. When you approach networking with an attitude of "How can I help (now or in the future)?" instead of "Here's what I do," you can offer advice, information, or referrals based on what others need, not based on your own agenda. When the phone rings, be prepared to offer help, and, if you cannot help right now, let the caller know how you will be available in the future.

Don't make assumptions about what people want; ask them. One woman I know ends every call with "Now, how can I help you?" Even if you don't offer help in the moment, follow her example; never walk away from a net-working opportunity without saying, "Keep me in mind if there is a way I can help you now or in the future." Then be sure to follow through.

Remember our lessons about responsibility and make sure you promise only what you can deliver, in terms of both actions and timeline. If you share information, stick with what you know; one difference between being a key member of someone's knowledge network and being seen as a know-it-all lies in recognizing your talents and your limits. If you offer to do something, think about the scope of the commitment. What do you want to do? What did you offer to do? Can you do it? Will you do it? When will you do it?

Share Knowledge

Who are the "go-to" people in your network—the ones who have the repu-tation of having (or knowing where to find) the right answers and being willing to share them? The true measure of your networking success is not who or what you know. It's how you share what you know with others. Steven Berglas recognized this in his article, "The Death of Status."

> "Today businesses are ruled by knowledge and responsiveness both to customers' needs and to rapid changes in the marketplace. Conse-quently, holding the key to information—not to the executive wash-room—connotes status. You can tell how much you matter in an organization by counting the number of questions you're asked, e-mail messages or calls you receive, and decisions you're involved in."

In fact, there are two kinds of people who are indispensable. One kind corners the market on some knowledge or skill and, in effect, holds the or-ganization hostage. The other kind is dedicated to making the organization run more effectively, and has more long-term staying power. These people see the big picture. They spend time developing new employees and plan-ning new business strategies. They know that the best way to get promoted is to train someone to do their job. This attitude leads to a new definition of status that makes hoarding knowledge unnecessary. Knowledge is not a zero-sum game; on the contrary, sharing knowledge builds a natural support system based on what people know. A person who shares knowledge can transform strangers and competitors into colleagues and customers into partners. When you are recognized as a contributor and an information sharer, you can, in turn, tap into your network and be among the first to learn the latest information. When you receive a valuable piece of information return the favor by thinking about which people in your network can use it. Be knowledgeable about obstacles as well as opportunities so that people won't be hit broadside with information for which they could have been prepared. When you are known for your ideas and for sharing your knowledge, people will take your calls, give you their time, and answer your questions. They will seek you out because they want to, not because they have to, or because such-and-such policy tells them to, or because they need your permission. They tell you openly what is going on because they see you as a resource and they know they will leave the encounter with new ideas and information.

Strive to add value to every connection you make.

Another great way to be a resource is to use your IOU list. As you meet new people or review your existing network, make a note of the kinds of information that might be of use to each person. List how you might be able to help each person in your network. Think about their interests, their industries, and other areas of their lives. Then make it a practice to check your list regularly. I guarantee you will read, hear, or learn something of value you can pass on to them. When you do, send a "Keeping You Informed" note card (I also call it a "KYI"), a format I designed as a personal way of saying "I'm just keeping in touch."

Become a Bridge

Probably the most important way you can reach out to others is by helping them access your network. In 1929, Hungarian author Frigyes Karinthy first proposed the idea that everyone in the world is connected through a web of acquaintances, with each person being at most six steps away from any other person. The "six degrees of separation" became a popular parlor game after the 1993 film with that name (most of us have played the "Six Degrees of Kevin Bacon"), but it is, in fact, a powerful networking reality. Your network is connected to the networks of others; this means you can build a bridge from the people you know to the people that others know. You become someone who knows someone who knows someone. And that makes you a valuable "bridge" for them and a center of influence.

When you extend yourself to help others by extending your network for them, you can become a matchmaker. Authentic networkers live by the words "You've got to get in touch with so-and-so—she can help you." When you introduce people, point out the ways you think they can be helpful to one another. Keep notes of these introductions and follow up later to see how they worked out.

Give Back

Every marketplace has a currency that allows participants to make exchanges and to build up value in their respective "bank accounts." Your networking currency is what you offer through your knowledge, your expertise, and your connections. And in the networking marketplace, the "exchange rate" you enjoy is largely influenced by the value you offer to others and by the graciousness with which you offer your resources.

If you are like most people, you are more aware of what you have given than what you have received. You know the credit side of your account book very well but keep track less accurately of the debit side. When giving to others, you may fear they will take too much, or take advantage of you. You may not trust the reciprocity principle to work in every case. And you know what? You are right—some people will use you. Some will never thank you. Oh well, so what? That doesn't matter when your actions come from within, from who you are, not how you want to be seen, and when the level of giving is right for the relationship. The same balance applies when you are granting requests as when you are asking for help: Anything you give has to fit in the context of the relationship. Understanding that, you will naturally prioritize and help people in your core network or your strong professional friends more than you will distant acquaintances. And use common sense: Give *very* sparingly to people who have a sense of entitlement and assume that things are automatically owed to them.

Being a resource means you are available to assist as well as to be assisted.

One way to participate in the "generalized exchange" is to give back to the community through volunteering. It is fitting that volunteering is mentioned in the first lesson, on responsibility, and now comes full circle in this final lesson, on reaching out. Volunteering takes us out of ourselves by reminding us that our needs are not greater than the needs of others. It helps us through transitions and brings about sharing and connecting with others. Successful people serve the community through active participation in charitable, social, and cultural groups. They do good by giving something back. They understand the power of connections at a different level, and networking becomes a lifelong process. As a client of mine said, once you become a resource to others, you understand that life is one big network.

THE BENEFITS OF REACHING OUT

Reaching out enhances your ability to network in many ways. It fosters the best kind of reputation, one in which you are known for helping, rather than for your current job expertise. This earns a place for you in the networks of other people. Reaching out to others also strengthens relationships by building goodwill when you offer your support.

There are other, less obvious benefits to giving back. One of the great surprises of recent scientific research is that giving—of either money or time— not only makes you feel good, it can actually improve your health. Generous people are happier, are healthier, and may even live longer than they would have if they were less giving. Most people feel great satisfaction through helping others, even to the point of experiencing a "helper's high," brain activity that is visible on an MRI scan. The helper's high is associated with dopamine, the same feel-good chemical that kicks in when you *receive* money. Having something to offer can give you a real psychological boost. Reaching out moves you from feeling or being seen as helpless, to a condition of helpfulness. And yes, you do have plenty to offer, every day—ideas, insight, or just a willing ear—no matter where you are in your career. Never underestimate your potential for helping and having a positive impact. If you focus your energy where you can make a difference,

Your networking currency is what you offer through your knowledge, your expertise, and your connections.

you won't feel that you are always asking and never giving. Even if you have nothing to give in return at that moment, networking is not about owing anybody or keeping tabs. Sometimes your contacts will simply experience the satisfaction of having helped you on your journey. That in itself is a gift.

Truly helpful people have no expectation of benefits, but the principle of reciprocity generally returns their favors, often in unexpected ways. For example, my nephews had a high school football coach whose philosophy was simple: "I really believe in helping people." As one of his student athletes commented, "Whenever he saw somebody in need, he tried to help. Whenever he was in the position to help somebody, he did. It's not really a complicated philosophy of life, but it's a hard one to live up to." The football coach wanted field lighting so that his team could play night games at home, but there was no money in the budget to cover the expense. He sent an e-mail to his team alumni mentioning the need. Within a week more than enough money was contributed to light the field. That's a network!

Those lights are the smallest part of that coach's legacy. What do you want your legacy to be? Authentic networkers want to be remembered for the attitude, abilities, and actions that helped others find their way and attain their goals. Reaching out helps you create the kind of network you want. A great network has no boundaries and can last a lifetime. You never know where it will take you until you reach out, and then you will experience things you would never have had the opportunity to do before.

"Help others to succeed and you too will succeed" has become a business truism. Be one of the people who have helped others along the way.

Questions for Reflection

▷ Who in your network comes to mind as someone who is known as a resource to others? What does this person do that is different?

▷ Think of three people you want to know better. Over the next week, think of one way you could help each of them.

▷ Have you recently given help, information, or a referral to someone? What was the outcome?

▷ Whom can you help right now?

RECAP
Putting It All Together

DO YOU REMEMBER the "typical week" I described at the beginning of this book? During that trip to Washington, D.C., I made several connections, some of which have been lasting ones, all in the course of my normal day. Let's look at them again in light of the seven lessons of authentic networking described in this book.

When I attended the presentations without my friends and approached the well-known author after the conference session, I was taking *responsibility* for myself and moving past my natural reluctance to talk with strangers. Later, when I introduced her to someone in my network who could help her, I was *reaching out*—becoming a valued resource by extending my network.

When the woman who shared my cab recognized my name and told me she had been planning to call me for counseling, this was my *reputation* at work.

When I explored the option of hiring a car to the airport, and then took the driver's business card, I was engaging in *research*. And when I passed the information on to my neighbor, I was *reaching out* to share what I had learned and strengthening a *relationship*.

When I talked with George on the flight home, I was building *rapport*. When I shared resources he might want to consider in his upcoming transition, I was sharing my knowledge and *reaching out* again.

Authentic networking has, for me, become a *habit* that regularly benefits me and the many people I encounter. You can accomplish the same thing by consciously incorporating the seven lessons described in this book into your day-to-day attitude and activities. Over time, those lessons will be become a genuine part of how you operate when meeting and networking with others.

You may be thinking, "That makes sense, but how can I do that?" Well, let's look for advice again from Benjamin Franklin and his approach to self-improvement. Franklin did not have access to the research we cited in the Responsibility lesson, suggesting that anyone can create a new habit with twenty-one days of practice. But he well understood that he could improve himself through practicing the qualities he desired. To that end, Franklin committed himself to a personal improvement program, identifying thirteen "virtues" that he wanted to adhere to. He created a chart, listing the qualities he wished to foster in himself and the days of the week. At the end of each day he evaluated himself, and placed a mark indicating his success in each area.

> *Make networking a habit that will serve you and the people who matter to you.*

Franklin's attempt as a young man to make a habit of what he called the "thirteen virtues" provides a practical twenty-first century model for how each of us can incorporate the seven lessons of *The Power of Everyday Networking* in our daily lives. Here is a snapshot view of the seven lessons.

▷ **Lesson 1—Responsibility:** Take personal responsibility for managing your career and maintaining connections.

▷ **Lesson 2—Reputation:** Build a reputation you can be proud of, one you will want others to share with their own networks.

▷ **Lesson 3—Relationships:** Develop genuine and long-lasting relationships by taking a sincere interest in others.

▷ **Lesson 4—Rapport:** Establish rapport. The strength of your network—bonds built on rapport—matters more than its size.

▷ **Lesson 5—Requirements:** Master the rules of the road of networking. Follow networking protocols and best practices by treating people and their time with respect.

▷ **Lesson 6—Research:** Do your research, using traditional tools, modern technology, and especially your network as resources.

▷ **Lesson 7—Reaching Out:** Reach out and become a valuable resource for others. Authentic networkers are reciprocators; they give support and help whenever, wherever, and in whatever ways they can, without keeping score.

Now arrange these lessons on a chart such as the one that follows. Make several copies so that you can practice for at least twenty-one days!

	Sunday	Monday	Tuesday	Wednesday	Thursday	Friday	Saturday
Responsibility							
Reputation							
Relationships							
Rapport							
Requirements							
Research							
Reaching out							

Every evening, take a minute to think about your networking actions of the day. You may want to focus on one lesson during one week and a different lesson at another time. The point is to practice your new behaviors so that the habits of authentic networking can become a routine part of your life.

Remember the principles of authentic networking.
- ▷ Networking is a skill that can be learned. It needs to be practiced, and then it becomes a habit, until finally it feels "natural."
- ▷ A network is earned through effort. It doesn't just happen.
- ▷ A network is useful only when it serves its members. Networks are designed to be tapped and shared.

When you hold yourself accountable for your new behaviors, you begin to live by these principles. My "typical" week demonstrates that it is possible to make networking a habit that will serve you and the people who matter to you. Whether you develop a self-improvement program or simply start every day with an open attitude and a who-can-I-help-today approach to work and life, the authentic you will emerge in your networking efforts. You can earn a strong network that will benefit all its members. When you practice what you have learned in this book, you will soon see how the seven lessons interact and naturally build on one another. Before you know it, people may be calling you a networking guru too!

NOTES

Page 5: Herminia Ibarra's comments were quoted by Cybele Weisser in "7 steps to get your finances back on track," CNNmoney.com, April 9, 2010. Available online at http://money.cnn.com/2010/03/30/pf/fix_finances.moneymag/index.htm.

Page 9: Matt Lauer's interview with U.S. first lady Michelle Obama appeared on the *Today Show* (MSNBC, New York) on February 3, 2010.

Page 17: Peter Drucker's comments appeared in his article, "Managing Oneself," in the January 2005 issue of *Harvard Business Review*.

Julie Mannion was quoted by Alison Baenen in "KCD's Julie Mannion turns designer dreams into runway reality," *Harper's Bazaar*, Fall/Winter 2010. p. 87.

David Maister. 1997. *True Professionalism* (New York: Free Press).

Page 20: Deiric McCann spoke in the July 1984 issue of *Cara*, the Aer Lingus in-flight magazine.

Page 22: "Pick Yourself Up" lyrics from the 1936 film *Swing Time.* Lyrics by Dorothy Fields; music by Jerome Kern.

Page 29: Jack Welch was quoted by Anne Fisher in "The Trouble with MBAs," *Fortune*, April 30, 2007, pp. 49–50.

Page 40: Selwyn Raab, "Donovan Cleared of Fraud Charges by Jury in Bronx," *New York Times,* May 26, 1987; available at .nytimes.com/gst/fullpage.html?res=9B0DE5DE1031F935A15756C0A961948260

Page 45: The statistics about Internet use come from www.internetworldstats. com.

Page 46: Rosabeth Moss Kanter. 1995. *World Class*. (New York: Simon and Schuster). P. 87.

Page 49: Judith Viorst. 1998. *Necessary Losses* (New York: Simon & Shuster). pp. 179-181.

Page 51: John Glenn was quoted in *Newsweek*, December 28, 1998, p. 59.

Page 54: Laura Pedersen's article, "Petworking," appeared in the *New York Times*, October 22, 2000. Available online at www.nytimes.com/2000/10/22/ nyregion/petworking.html?scp=1&sq=petworking&st=nyt.

Page 56: The story about Aydin Senkut and Elad Gil appeared in "And Google Begat . . . The search giant's former employees are seeding tech startups—and shaping another wave of innovation," by Spencer E. Ante and Kimberly Weisul, *Bloomberg Businessweek*, March 8, 2010, p. 39.

The story about Dan Schawbel appeared in "You, 2.0," by Nick Cunkelman, *Boston Globe Sunday Magazine*, August 22, 2010, p. 5.

Page 61: The Q&A appeared in "Tongue-tied when networking? Develop foundation for dialogue," by Perry Capell, *The Wall Street Journal*, Career Q&A, June 6, 2006, p. x.

Page 62: Bob Burg. 1994. *Endless Referrals* (New York: McGraw-Hill).

Page 67: Information on Ben Franklin is from "The Autobiography of Benjamin Franklin." Available at www.ushistory.org/franklin/autobiography/ page48.htm.

Page 72: Edward M. Hallowell, "The Human Moment at Work," *Harvard Business Review*, January 1, 1999.

Page 79: Peter Post is quoted in Andrea Sachs, "Manners Matter." Available online at www.dountoothers.org/manners50807.html.

Page 88: Bill Gates' comment on Knowledge and power comes from: Bill Gates with Collins Hemingway. 1999. *Business @ The Speed of Thought (Using a digital nervous system)*, (New York: Time Warner), p. 240.

Page 94: The Webgrrls story appeared in "Get your career in Site," Gina Imperato, *Fast Company*, February 29, 200, and can be found at http://www. fastcompany.com/magazine/32/atwork.html?page=0%2C4.

Page 97: The Charles Schwab story was recounted by Maria Bartiromo, "To Tell the Truth." Available online at www.rd. com/money-makers-to-tell-the-truth/ article28188.html.

Page 104: Wikipedia. "Pay it forward." Available online at http://en.wikipedia. org/wiki/Pay_it_forward.

Ralph Waldo Emerson's 1841 essay, "Compensation," is widely available in print and online.

Page 107: Steven Berglas. "The Death of Status." *Inc. Magazine* (October 1996).

Page 110: For discussion of physiological effects of giving, see: Stephen Post. 2008. *Why Good Things Happen to Good People* (New York: Broadway).